the enlightened response

To Colin

Enjoy the Journey!

Ross

the enlightened response

Leatham Green,
Head of Organisational Development,
East Sussex County Council
'It is always exciting when you come across someone or something that changes your view of life. To describe Ross, his book and his workshops in such a way is no exaggeration. He challenges your habitual behaviour in an encouraging way, he supports you with empathy and above all makes everything seem possible through the liberal application of good humour and fun.'

Pete Brown,
Board Director, Bywater plc,
International Management Consulting.
'This book contains The Grand Unified Theory of Life – it has it all.'

Elaine Taylor,
Ericsson Global Master Trainer
'Ross has a unique style, personality and creative approach. His depth of personal and professional experience enables him to write and present in a way that is both entertaining and practical.'

Jeff Turnbull,
'MacDonalds' Recruiting, London
'Ross is highly motivated, dynamic and extremely professional'

Sal Barbagello,
Manager Retail Training, Australia Post, Brisbane
'Ross' style of teaching creates an ideal learning environment…'

Brendan Long,
General Manager Camp Eden Health Retreat, Australia
'Ross's work has been acclaimed by many as a major turning point in their lives.'

Mike Willesee,
Journalist and TV presenter
'… professional and personable…'
'… Ross succeeds in connecting with each individual.'

the
enlightened
response

'Create the life you want –
moment to moment, choice by choice'

Ross Page

A
NUTSHELL
IMPRINT

To all the wonderful people
who have shared my life journey thus far.
Of course these number in the millions by now
and some of you know who you are.

The major players in the creation of this book are:

Anthony Tindale   – who sometimes had more faith in me than I did.
Christiaan Page   – who taught and teaches me to focus.
Pete Brown   – who only sees wisdom in me because it is a reflection.
Dr Hilda Des Arts – who taught me to 'Live, love, learn and leave a legacy.'

And especially my wife, Diane, who lives, loves and learns with me and with whom I share my love and my life.

First published in 2002 by Nutshell

Nutshell
Metro House, Northgate
Chichester, West Sussex PO19 1SD

Website: www.enlightenedresponse.com
Email: info@enlightenedresponse.com

ISBN 0-9542630-0-6

The British Library Cataloguing in Publication Data.
A catalogue record for this book is available from the British Library.

Designed and typeset in Joanna, Poppl Laudatio and Helvetica by
EVERGREEN GRAPHICS 11 The Drive, Craigweil on Sea, Aldwick, West Sussex PO21 4DU.

Edited by BROWNS EDITING SERVICE.

Printed and bound in Great Britain by ANTONY ROWE.

All illustrations and photographs by ROSS PAGE.

CONTENTS

Mantras and Chanting

Object Focus

Visualisations

13 Creating Peace in my Relationships

14 What is an Enlightened Response?

15 And finally…

≈≈

INTRODUCTION

What part do we play in the creation of the events in our lives? How do we create wealth and poverty, loving relationships and destructive relationships, war and peace, relaxation and stress?

What if it was as simple as learning to respond, rather than react?

- Are there ever times when you wish you could stop rushing and worrying, and just enjoy life?
- Do you sometimes wish you had stopped to think before you opened your mouth?
- If your health and lifestyle were depicted in the shape of a wheel, would you sometimes wonder how it got so out of balance?
- And do you often doubt that your hopes and dreams will ever be fulfilled?

'If you want to create more in your life – more happiness, better relationships, improved health, increased wealth, or all the above – then read on. You already use some of the methods. The Enlightened Response could help you to fine-tune those methods, enabling you to live the happy and rewarding life you may have dreamed about, but wondered how to achieve.'

We have all had enlightened responses to things that happen in our lives. They are the times when we walk away from a situation with that warm, reassuring feeling that we have just done or said exactly the right thing for the occasion, or have at least performed to the best of our ability. What if we could learn to have more of these Enlightened Responses and fewer 'knee-jerk' reactions?

Personal or corporate, financial or spiritual, the principles are exactly the same. All too often in the past my reactions to the challenges of life and business have been unplanned and habitual. Enlightened Responses have allowed me to choose from moment to moment the shape, direction and content of my life.

REACTION IS HABITUAL
RESPONSE IS EFFECTIVE
ENLIGHTENED RESPONSE
IS POWERFUL AND CREATIVE

Our lives, viewed through our senses and our own perception filters, are really nothing else except EXPECTATIONS, EVENTS and EVALUATIONS. It is a continual process we experience every minute of every day. Our lives only exist in our thoughts. Without our thoughts about these *3 E's of Life*, do we really have a life?

In The Enlightened Response I have outlined a set of tools for improving our ability to observe our personal expectations, events and evaluations to a point where we begin to understand how we create our lives and our world.

> **Self Observation** creates **Awareness**.

> **Awareness** is the main ingredient of **Creative Expectation**.

> **Creative Expectations** lead to **Enlightened Responses**.

> **Enlightened Responses** can change lives and change the world.

Through understanding and utilising this simple process we can create a wide range of outcomes including:

- calm and harmony
- fulfilling personal relationships
- understanding of our spirituality
- a more rewarding career
- material possessions and investments
- travel

The events we create can be as varied as the expectations, which precede them.

Why choose Enlightened Responses?

'An Enlightened Response is a conscious choice to respond, rather than react, to anything that happens in your life.'

- We ask children to choose Enlightened Responses when we plead with them to think before they act.
- We expect our doctors to prescribe Enlightened Responses based on objective diagnosis of our symptoms.
- And we hope that our leaders will choose Enlightened Responses, based on awareness of the facts, before they spend our taxes or plunge us into war.

Every action we choose to take is preceded by a thought process. The Enlightened Response technique will enable us to effectively intervene between our own thoughts and actions – create a PAUSE button if you like – allowing time to select appropriate and more effective responses.

In the corporate world, no matter if you're buying, selling, managing or presenting, Enlightened Responses can mean clearer thinking, faster decision-making and an ability to choose the most effective response to any business challenge.

The Enlightened Response **is more than about creating balance** _amidst_ **the turmoil of our lives.**

It's more than about creating balance _in spite of_ **the turmoil of our lives.**

It is about creating balance _because of_ **the turmoil of our lives and accepting the inevitability of constant change.**

How to read this book

I need to warn you about something. My work, whether in the training room or in print, has a strong personal bias. To the eternal wonderment and sometimes chagrin of my colleagues, I am continually drawing metaphorical links between my life experiences and the principles and models that we expound. Mine is a simple, or some say a childlike, view of the world, and I am complimented if this is the impression I have given. Children see experiences as what they are – effective or ineffective. We teach them to judge these simple experiences as good or bad, and therefore limit their potential for learning. I would rather see my experiences, on reflection, as learning tools, having neither a positive nor negative value.

'I' have written this book with an emphasis on the very word with which 'I' started this sentence. Try as I might and with all the awareness I can muster, 'I' can still only look at the world from 'my' point of view and filtered through my own genetic filter and life experiences. I do not seek to denigrate all the fabulous work done by hundreds of self-help authors who choose to write from what I call a teachers perspective. As I first began to formulate my ideas into book form, a good friend suggested that I should write in the same manner as I present – in the first person. Consequently, my workshops and writings are generously embellished with illustrative stories and anecdotes from my own experiences of life – and for this I make no apology. I believe, in the final analysis, that we all make sense of the world through our own individual learning processes and not on the say so of any teacher, presenter or author. Of course we are all influenced, to varying degrees, by role models, gurus, advisors, lecturers and facilitators, but in the end we make up our own minds.

I am passionate about my life and the path through, across, around, under and because of it. You do not have my inherited characteristics, nor have you followed my life path, so how can I possibly expect you to learn in exactly the same way as I have. You have been blessed with your own incredible genetic cocktail and a fascinating array of real life situations to explore. I do not want to impose my learning process on you or tell you what you should do, but merely tell my stories from which you may note some similarities and could, if you wanted to, choose to shape your own learning process.

Enough said. And now 'I' want to tell you about the time 'I'…

And some final pieces of advice before we launch into Chapter 1. I will assume that if you have purchased this book or have acquired it by any other means, that you have the basic skills required to read it, but a few tips on the structure of the text and the intentions of the author may increase your enjoyment.

The chapters do have a logical progression, or at least that was my aim. That doesn't mean to say that you won't gain benefit from just diving in at any point. Although there is a common theme, there are many separate subjects covered. It is my hope that each chapter is capable of standing alone as an explanation of a string of ideas, along with a set of suggestions for applying these ideas to improve the quality of your life.

And what is the common theme?

The Enlightened Response endeavours to answer the following questions:

- What are Enlightened Responses?
- How can Enlightened Responses increase our effectiveness and enjoyment?
- How can we create more of them?

I have also added two features to facilitate the learning process.

1. And in <u>YOUR</u> life…

Knowledge on its own, without a plan for its practical application, is not all that useful. In an effort to personalise your learning process I have included some suggestions at the end of each chapter on how you might apply the theories in your own back yard. Of course, life will surely be less tumultuous if certain ground rules are adhered to, cultural norms acknowledged and social conventions followed; but there is still plenty of scope for doing life in your own way. In the spirit of the once fashionable *choose your own ending* genre of books, this is where I encourage you to *write your own script*. You are directing this comedic drama, as well as playing the lead. Take a close look at your personal soap opera and start deciding which bits you will screen and which will end up on the editing floor.

2. In thirty words or less…

Confronted with a client or workshop participant who is finding it difficult to clearly and concisely encapsulate their issue or problem, I often resort to the *in ten words or less* technique. Quite simply, I ask them to state the main points or theme in a limited number of words. Ten is a mid-range restriction – sometimes I allow them as few as one or as many as twenty, but the principle is the same. Restriction in any form and in any aspect of our lives forces us to be more creative with the resources we have. Hence the saying, 'Necessity is the mother of invention'. Asking people to summarise their views into a tight package encourages them to remove the embellishments and the rambling and cut to the chase.

If you were sitting with a group of friends and noticed that the building was on fire, would you say:

a) 'Excuse me chaps, but it has come to my attention, and of course this is purely my perception, that the construction in which we are currently housed is in imminent risk of being destroyed through the rapid disintegration of the combustible materials of which it is fabricated.'

Or, in five words or less

b) 'Fire! Quick, get out!'

In an effort to translate this 'in ten words or less' technique into written form, I will include a text box at the end of each chapter that will summarise its essence. Invoking the powers of Author's License, and because each chapter covers several topics, I have allowed myself the luxury of using thirty words or less. This summary statement is meant as an aid to understanding how we can employ Enlightened Responses to help us achieve success in every area of our lives.

So… read from cover to cover or pick a line, page or chapter at random, but however you choose to extract the information contained herein, I hope this book brings you enjoyment as well knowledge.

And in <u>YOUR</u> life...

1. Be aware of your own personal bias as you read. Are you trying to prove me wrong or right? Are you the sort of person who looks for things that work or things that don't work? What other biases do you have?

2. Please don't think how good the information in this book would be for someone else. These ideas and concepts work; but don't take my word for it. Test them by applying them to your own life.

INTRODUCTION
IN THIRTY WORDS OR LESS...

'Self observation, awareness and managing our expectations empowers us to select more
Enlightened Responses
and so create the life we want – moment to moment, choice by choice.'

---

*'It does not serve me
to plant corn,
then wish for potatoes'*

CHAPTER ONE

SELF OBSERVATION – IN PRINCIPLE

*'In the fields of observation,
chance favours only the prepared mind.'*

LOUIS PASTEUR

Challenges

It would seem that from the moment ova and sperm begin their respective journeys, life becomes a continual challenge. Month after month a female's eggs will end up discarded and billions of tiny male tadpoles, although to no such strict timetable, experience a similar fate. My conception and yours were results of intense competition and both were miraculous events.

I was subsequently born into a mostly affluent section of western society, but still I marvel that I survived my childhood and adolescence virtually unscathed. And now as an adult I fight never-ending battles against workloads, traffic and the rigours of parenting. So why am I so surprised that the wheels of my life rarely turn smoothly? Just being aware that this winding and potholed road is normal can lead to a relieving of the pressure I often feel to be perfect.

Some of the later chapters of this book deal with deepening an understanding of why we often feel stressed and why we find our lives so challenging. But maybe it is not always the challenge itself which constitutes our greatest obstacle. It could have more to do with our perceptions of the challenge. Perhaps if we saw our lives as something to be enjoyed, not endured; an adventure to be experienced and not a problem to be solved; we could maybe lighten up and enjoy the scenery. How much more effective would we be if we could choose each and every response we make rather than stumble blindly into an automatic reaction? It is a rhetorical question of course and one that

you will probably assume I have my own answer to; and you will be right.

One method

I will offer ONE (and only one) simple and important technique to learn and practise, and then suggest fifty ways, and thousands of variations, for using it in our daily lives. But I am assuming here that this one, marvellous technique, is something that you want. I need to get some sort of agreement with you that we (you, me, and a few billion others on this planet) could use some type of method for calming and focussing our minds and our thought processes. There is mounting evidence which suggests that, as a species, we need to be seeking out more pathways to health and well-being. And I'm not going to reinvent the wheel here, as such a pathway already exists. Self Observation, in myriad different forms, has been part of man's culture for thousands (and perhaps millions) of years. Mind control, prayer, chanting, yoga, tai chi, dance, drugs, meditation and music are just some of the methods that have been used to tame our thinking and pacify the warring tribes in our own heads.

For many of us, peaceful surroundings can aid us to create inner peace and balance. A holiday in The Bahamas, two weeks at a mountain retreat, a relaxing weekend with family and friends... but in a world where we are constantly bombarded with information, distractions and obstacles, it is hardly practical to suggest that to gain that peace and focus, we need to start by eliminating sensory stimuli and live on a permanent vacation. I remember being back in the office, only two days after a four week break, and trying hard to recall if I'd really had a holiday or had I only dreamed it.

Self Observation can assist us to create that relaxed holiday feeling within us, regardless of our surroundings or situation and without us losing focus or reducing our effectiveness as individuals or as members of the community. In other words it won't require that you join a sect, shave your head, quit your job, alienate your family and friends or outlay inordinate amounts of time or money on tapes, equipment or more books. Each of us has been adequately endowed with all the faculties we need to bring about peace and prosperity in our lives, and every day is furnished with an abundance of opportunities with which we can experiment and practise.

We will be looking at these opportunities in more detail a bit later and analysing how they can stimulate us to respond in various ways – ways in which we may have a lot more choice than we previously might have thought. It makes sense to me that if these stimuli are to be our constant companions, especially in the city, e.g. traffic, noise crowds, then why not incorporate these so called distractions into our lives, accept their inevitability and become aware of how they can move us forward, not hold us back. Instead of *distractions from* our environment, we'll look at ways of accepting them as *part of* our environment – a sort of 'If you can't beat 'em, join 'em' mentality!

What is Self Observation?

Left to their own devices our thoughts will often feel a need to classify themselves either positive or negative; bounce back and forth, comparing themselves with the past and postulating about the future; and cap it off with an habitual reaction.

Practising Self Observation will teach us to be more objective and enable us to stand back momentarily and make enlightened decisions i.e. decisions made with a clearer understanding of the way our thought processes work. The resultant responses are more likely to be ones we have chosen, not those forced upon us by routine or custom.

For the purpose of clarity I will be using the term Self Observation in this book as a generic term to cover any form of Mind Stilling, Thought Focus, Meditation, Visualisation, except of course when quoting another source or discussing a particular method which falls under the Self Observation heading.

For example, in my quest to discover how different cultures have tackled the restless mind problem, I visited a Tibetan Buddhist monastery in Darjeeling, Northern India. After the early morning prayers and chanting rituals and over a cup of steaming, salted, buttermilk tea (an acquired taste!) I asked one of the monks how he *meditated*, as this was the term with which he was most familiar.

> 'My friend,' he calmly replied,
> 'my whole life is a meditation.'

Sitting on the steps of the beautiful and colourful eighteenth century

monastery, bathed by warm spring sunshine and gazing out over tranquil tea plantations towards the towering snowcaps of the high Himalaya, with the distant, slightly musical sounds of children playing; it wasn't difficult to believe that this particular life could be a perpetual meditation. 'But what about *my* life Lama?' (teacher) I asked. 'What about a life in the city, or in a war zone or even in the tumult of a family household amid chores, careers and mortgages?'

My robed friend patiently went on to explain that his life had not always been this idyllic, and indeed still wasn't always so. Tales of fleeing from his homeland in Tibet under gunfire, painful separations from family and friends and stories of establishing a new life in a foreign land, were all delivered with the a tone of calm acceptance that said, 'It's no use complaining that life is not what I want it to be. I will work with and appreciate what I have'. One of his sayings that I particularly liked, translates roughly to;

> **'It does not serve me to plant corn,**
> **then wish for potatoes'**

There's no such thing as a bad day

Every facet of his life, when viewed with a gentle focus and acceptance, could be a focal point for peaceful observation. Observation and focus without judgement. To my Buddhist companion there was no such thing as a good day or a bad day. A sunny day was just that – a sunny day. A rainy day was similarly accepted as just another day. With no expectation, and then no judgement, there was no need for a rainy day to disappoint him, as he accepted it just the way it was presented to him.

He had no need to distinguish between relaxing sounds and tranquil sounds. He had no need to judge them good sounds or bad sounds. He merely accepted them as they were; just sounds. They might be loud sounds or soft sounds, harsh sounds or gentle sounds; slow sounds or fast sounds, but as far as possible (by his own admission he hadn't perfected it yet) they weren't awarded a value – a *goodness* or *badness* value, if you like.

'Doesn't this make life boring?' I hear some people ask. Well, not to him. Through his eyes, life was just one continuous and amazing

Ross with Tibetan Buddhist monks. Bhutia Busty monastery, Darjeeling 1998.

string of miracles. Could we too learn to see it that way? The fact that we lay down and go into a state of suspended animation for six to eight hours every night and then wake up again in the morning is an absolute miracle when you really think about it. Is that boring? He had merely taught himself to appreciate every moment, every ability, every situation, every sight and sound. What he refers to as Meditation, I will be calling Self Observation. A life lived in perpetual amazement at our existence, and the beauty, wonder and challenges of our daily lives, could hardly ever be referred to as boring. 'Ah yes' you may ask, 'But is he *happy*?'

Happiness; a natural or induced state?

Some things don't travel very well from one culture to another, and the Eastern concept of happiness would seem a perfect example. In Western culture, we tend to see happiness and sadness as a sliding scale with the midpoint being a sort of nothingness; neutrality depicted by an expressionless face. If something makes us happy, we smile, or if it makes us sad, we frown, but almost always we return at some point to the bland balance point. But what if – and I like to play the 'What if?' game – the midpoint could be shifted slightly left of centre towards *contentment*?

What if, when in standby mode, we defaulted to a state of mild amusement in regard to our lives instead of a state of sensory limbo? This is what I have assessed as one of the primary differences between the Eastern and Western quest for Nirvana. Perhaps it is the explanation for the ever present, bemused half-smile of many Eastern holy men. I know for me personally (and I can only possibly see the world through my own filter), when I stop playing the 'I'll be happy when...' game and start seeing the events of the world around me as a constant source of interest and fascination, I begin to experience my life with an attitude of gratitude rather than one of resigned numbness.

Is Self Observation a tool for creating happiness and contentment, or any other name we like to allot to that blissful state in which most of us aspire to live? In a way I guess the answer is 'Yes!' But, and I may be splitting hairs here, I would prefer to see it as a technique for helping us to recognise that state of happiness which I believe dwells in all of us and often lurks just below the surface. Happiness is a state of mind, not a product of circumstance. Self Observation is a simple, tried and tested tool for helping us to unleash our potential for contentment and peace of mind, no matter what our particular circumstances may be.

Fitting a PAUSE Button

Skilfully observing the way you interact with your world will enable you to fit a PAUSE button to your life. Once activated, the pause will give you time to evaluate your thoughts more effectively and then move on to choose appropriate responses rather than reactions born of habit. Once mastered, the feelings of calm and clarity created will provide respite from the stress that comes from constant cycles of *thought* to *reaction* and back to *thought* again. Self Observation will lead you to *awareness*. Sometimes just realising there is a problem, knowing what it is and how it got there, can make a world of difference. If nothing else, it's a great starting point. Awareness is the switch for activating your personal pause button, allowing you to view your life in what seems like slow motion – a succession of Expectations, Events and Evaluations.

The 3 E's of Life
What's going to happen?
What's happening?
What happened?

The way we perceive our lives can be simply divided into three major aspects:

- **Expectations**
- **Events**
- **Evaluations**

We tend to see the absence of success in our lives as a major cause of stress. We are stressed when things don't go the way we planned or expected, but the stress produced directly by the present moment is usually not a problem. Stress begins to grow when we start evaluating the present situation against a past event that produced undesirable results, or against the expectation that we had before the present situation. We then project those results into the future as a probable outcome.

If we could strengthen our resolve to stay focused on the desired outcome rather than playing re-runs of the past scenario, we would vastly increase our chances of achieving the result we want. The added bonus with this method is that we even feel better in the run-up to the anticipated event. As I will illustrate in a later chapter, it is thoughts, not events, which govern the way we feel about life.

As psychologist and philosopher John Dewey stated in his
TROUBLE THEORY:

*'Thinking happens when there is a mismatch between
what we expect and what we actually find.'*

And in <u>YOUR</u> life...

1. What are the challenges you currently have in your life? Choose a couple that you find particularly difficult and have labelled 'terrible' or 'a nightmare'. Now ask yourself the follow-up question, 'Compared to what?' On a scale of terribleness, where would you place this challenge?

2. Do you only get that relaxed holiday feeling when you are on a holiday? How could you create more opportunities to experience these feelings more than for 3 or 4 weeks each year?

3. How often do you judge things, events or people as bad, and how does that make you feel?

4. Every time you feel irritated, stressed or angry, try to isolate the split second between thought and feeling by mentally pressing your PAUSE button.

OBSERVATION IN PRINCIPLE

IN THIRTY WORDS OR LESS...

'Objective observation, of self and by self, will build awareness, reduce judgement, increase happiness and allow us to pause momentarily before choosing **Enlightened Responses**.'

CHAPTER TWO

EXPECTATION

To-ing and Fro-ing

Most of us have experienced the panic of running late for work or an appointment. When I'm in such a predicament, there is always a voice in my head which starts to pre-play the conversation I'll be likely to have when I arrive: 'I'll say... and they'll probably say... but then I'll say... and if they don't like it they can...'

This Expectation then swings into an Evaluation of a past Event: 'The last time this happened I...' Then I'm back to an Expectation based on the Evaluation of the past Event: 'This time I'll be ready with...'

The facts of the moment – that I am sitting in an air-conditioned car on a beautiful sunny day with my favourite CD playing on the car stereo – have been completely obliterated by the mental gymnastics of tumbling from past to future and back again.

A couple of personal incidents illustrate this process on an everyday level. I shared a house with a close friend for a couple of years and we used to take turns at cooking dinner. Stir-fried vegetables was a favourite of mine, liberally doused with soy sauce, a sprinkle of ginger and always lots of fresh garlic. One particular night we'd run out of fresh garlic, so I scooped in a spoonful of the bottled minced variety. No problem; it tasted great. We both got what we expected and sat back to ponder what we could have for dessert. My housemate then disappeared into the kitchen, returning shortly with two bowls of a particularly smooth brand of caramel ice cream that we both enjoyed. You can imagine that my expectations were high as I spooned in the first mouthful, but the shock to my delicate and expectant taste buds was unbelievable. 'Aaahh – uurggh yuk,' I splurted as I ran to spit it out into the kitchen sink. 'What did you do to that?' I fully believed that I'd fallen foul of some cruel practical joke. It took a few minutes to work out that the clean spoon he had picked up to provide me with my dessert was somehow mixed up with the one I'd used to dispense the garlic!

What was the difference between the garlic I had enjoyed and savoured just ten minutes earlier and the garlic I was now choking on? Expectation.

A similar thing happened when another friend asked, as all good hosts do, if I'd like a hot drink. Apparently there was no tea, only coffee. Not being a regular coffee drinker, I reluctantly decided to have a cup, just to be sociable, thereby mentally preparing my taste buds for a coffee sensation rather than a tea sensation. 'Sugar?' she enquired. 'One thanks,' I replied, further preparing my flavour receptors. Now, the taste of coffee in lieu of tea I was prepared for. What came as a shock was the fact that she had inadvertently stirred in a teaspoon of salt. Another sprint to the sink!

This too was another example of stress being brought about by an inaccurate or inappropriate expectation.

Hope

A discussion with a colleague named Andy offered me yet another example of this process in action. His four-year-old son had been suffering terribly with eczema, an irritating and dispiriting skin complaint. Each night they would tuck him into bed expecting, based on many previous night's experience, that he would wake up crying and distressed some time during the night. 'Where does *hope* fit into this model?' Andy asked of me. 'I agree that we probably have an expectation, based on results, that he'll wake again, but we always hope that it will change.'

Hope is definitely an aspect of expectation, but I believe that it is an aspect of positive, creative expectation tinged with doubt. I can't help believing that if we have the strength of focus to align our expectations with strong mental images of our preferred outcome, we will more often than not reach these desired goals, whatever they may be.
I have heard it said: 'A wish is a goal without a plan for achieving it.' Perhaps a hope can be described as: 'a positive expectation coloured by the memory of negative outcomes.' Does this dark side of hope produce anxiety which in turn appears as eczema? It is a chicken and egg scenario. What does seem clear is that a deeply ingrained vision of the future – one you can see, taste, feel, smell – will stop or at least slow down the mind's tendency to bounce back and forth between past result and future expectation.

Let me repeat this in another way and in bold print:

'In our mostly threat free, sedentary lives there is very often NO STRESS in the Present Moment.'

Change your expectations and change your life

A few minutes quiet reflection will probably reveal that most of the things we worry about are either memories – often distorted by emotion and time – of something that did happen, or imagined scenarios of what could or might happen. Instead of just staying with the facts, our minds often search the past for a video-like recording of any similar situation we might have stored in the filing system. Then, anxious to either repeat – or in the running late scenario, probably not repeat – the results from the former event, we write a new script and project it into the future. This to-ing and fro-ing from past to future is often the cause of our stress. If we just stick with the truth of the situation i.e. 'I'm going to be late', without analysing past events and speculating on future ones, we can remain relatively calm in *What is*, not *What was* or *What will be*.

By dividing your experience of life into the three aspects of EXPECTATION, EVENT and EVALUATION, it then becomes a simple process to ascertain which of these aspects, if any, you have some control over.

And in <u>YOUR</u> life...

1. Watch for just how much (or little) time you spend in the present. When you feel anxious, is it because of something in the future, or memories of the past, or the stress of flitting back and forward between the two?

2. Do you hope for things to happen, or do you confidently expect them? Which do you think would be more effective? Make a list of the things you currently hope for and imagine upgrading them to expectations.

3. At some point each morning, spend at least a few moments examining your expectations for the day ahead. What do you expect to happen, who do you think will be there, how will the events affect you?

4. The following six questions, two for each of the 3 E's, form a quick and easy framework for taking control of your thinking and therefore your life. Take a moment now to remember some past experiences that did not turn out the way you had planned and ask yourself these questions in relation to it. Go on, try it!

- What was your EXPECTATION before the event?

- How could you have modified your EXPECTATION to increase your chance of success and therefore reduce your stress?

- What was your perception of the EVENT?

- How could you have changed the EVENT or at least have perceived it differently?

- What was your EVALUATION of the event?

- How could you have EVALUATED the event more positively and therefore reduce stress?

After practicing on past events, it is then only a short step to using these awarenesses before an event to create the results you desire. Following is an entire chapter devoted to this creative process that is based on awareness.

EXPECTATION

IN THIRTY WORDS OR LESS...

'By identifying the different types
of expectations we have, we can
begin to understand the way
in which we either create or experience
the events of our lives.'

CHAPTER THREE

THE CREATIVE POWER OF EXPECTATION

Our most energetic reactions to life's events seem to be reserved for those that fall furthest outside the realms of our expectation. Would it not make sense then for us to move more possibilities into these realms of expectation, therefore reducing the need to react?

We use sayings like, 'To be forewarned is to be forearmed' and we often hear people say, 'You know, I was half expecting it', when they are confronted with a sudden turn of events. 'This is just how I pictured it' is another common one, along with 'This is a dream come true', 'I knew that would happen', 'I thought I'd run into you here' and 'I had a feeling that...' Sound familiar?

So how much do our expectations govern our outcomes and results? Let's revisit the 3 E's model for a possible answer. We'll take the first element, EXPECTATION, and explore the possibility that by identifying the different types of expectation we have, we can begin to understand the way in which we either create or experience the events of our lives.

What started out as a book on Stress Management has slowly evolved into a 'how to' book on creating the life I want. The change in direction came about when I realised that, if I expect good things and set about actually creating them, then I have no need to feel stressed. Rather than focus on my problems it is far more effective to focus on the results I want to achieve.

Awareness as a Creative Tool

If the creation of desired outcomes is the end point of our daily existence, then *awareness* is the starting point of the adventure. Our lives are a continual creative process set in motion by our thoughts. Just as our minds link seemingly unrelated thoughts together in a never-ending stream, so too our lives can flow like a stream. As we learn the power of mentally creating the look and feel of our future, we are systematically devising a road map for our bodies to follow. Simple daily chores or complex visions of lifetime goals; our minds are equal to the task.

In its most recognisable form, we use this system to create the simplest necessities. If you are thirsty you will probably first of all acknowledge the message from your throat and tongue. You might then picture the range of options available to you – water from the tap, beer from the fridge, tea or coffee from a pot. The next step is picturing the route you will need to take to get to the kitchen, and then your body will physically follow this route map through to the point where the glass or cup is being lifted to your lips. And you use this system thousands of times every day, mostly without ever giving it a conscious thought.

If you want a free lesson in the clever use of Creative Expectations, spend some time watching children – they are masterful exponents of the process. Their lives are full of hopes, wishes and expectations which, when firmly set, initiate a vast range of responses in line with their goal. Of course they don't know much about goals and objectives, as they prefer to express these in terms of 'I want'.

'I want an ice cream!', 'I want a ride on the horsey!', 'I want THAT doll!' 'I want a BIG one / FAST one / RED one...' You can rest assured that the one you have will not be the one they want. But what is fascinating is the range of methods that will surface while they are in pursuit of their goal.

Asking – The casual approach
'Can I have it?' –.

The Polite Approach
'Please can I have it?'

Volume Enriched Asking
'DAD! I REALLY want it!

Pleading
Please, please, please can I have it?

Guilt Trip
> 'But you promised!'

Mean parent ploy
> 'You never let me have what I want.'

Bribery
> 'If I'm really good can I have it?'

Peer Comparison
> 'But Johnny's got one!'

Parent Comparison
> 'Josh's Dad bought *him* one.' (delivered with sad eyes)

Parent Play-off
> 'Come on Dad, Mum said I could have it'

Reverse Psychology
> 'Oh well, I didn't really want it anyway.' (with pout)

And a thousand other variations, but not forgetting the old favourites: Whinging, sulking, crying and the ever-reliable tantrum.

Adults can dream too

Maybe with some thought, we adults can also use this incredibly sophisticated tool to create all the results we wish for ourselves. Now might be a good time to look at these results and the internal process we go through in mentally preparing the way toward them. I believe that we generally get what we expect, but are there different levels of expectation and how do they influence the final result?

We all know someone who will always find a reason for something not to work. 'It'll be too big'. And then there's the person going one step further who will tell you ALL the reasons it won't work. 'It's too big, too slow, too square and too bright... and besides that, I personally don't like it.' Thank you for sharing! I have started with these two, as they seem to be the most commonly used and therefore the most easily recognised. Both are examples of what I call Obstructive Expectations, but how many categories are there?

Levels of expectation

Although there are possibly many different levels and varieties of expectation, I am just going to label five here to give you a feel for the concept. And for a few moments I would like to play the 'what if' game again and say… What if all our expectations (and we have millions of them) came under only FIVE major headings? And what if the vast creative canvas of my life could be shaped into a masterpiece simply by the understanding and clever use of my Creative Power of Expectation?

So what are these five headings and how do they impact on my life?

- **Multi Creative Expectation**
- **Creative Expectation**
- **Blind Expectation**
- **Obstructive Expectation**
- **Multi Obstructive Expectation**

I've found that one of the best ways of explaining this concept is to relate each level to the behaviour patterns of easily recognisable personalities in our lives. Please keep in mind though, that we ALL access the entire range of levels depending on our moods, the current state of our self-esteem or the particular task we are involved in. For the most part I believe I access my Multi-Creative expectations wherever possible, but in several areas of my life, notably mathematics, puzzles, machines and housework, I choose to have Multi Obstructive Expectations. Quite simply, I don't like these activities, I'm not very good at them (I'm not sure which of those comes first) and I will find a hundred valid reasons for avoiding them. So let's examine the five levels.

Multi Creative Expectation

It's probable that we have all met someone who plans their whole life around the ability to see a thousand options in every situation. Every waking moment is filled with endless possibilities and opportunities – and with each new opportunity comes another thousand options. This is the person who, when asked for an idea, will deliver a dozen. This is an attitude that makes things happen, but not always for the best. Focus can be a problem and energy dissipates as it is spread thinly to cover all the available choices.

Creative Expectation

This is the person who sits at a meeting with their one big idea of the year and is so focussed on the positive benefits of it that they simply can't see any other suggestions on the table. Focus is a strong suit for the creative expector but this causes a one eyed approach to life and to the realms of creative possibility.

Blind Expectation

The fence sitter. Nothing good to say, nothing bad to say and no personal axes to grind or flags to wave. Their language is characterised by phrases like, 'I didn't see that coming' and 'I never would have thought…' They live in foggy blur of what could happen and a state of perpetual astonishment about what just happened. Everything surprises them.

Obstructive Expectation

We all know the days when we are in this sort of mood and we all know someone who spends a lot of time there. These are the stubborn, 'only one answer and its mine' type of person. When an idea is placed on the table they will seize their opportunity to unleash all their pent up resentment on an innocent and inanimate object and anyone who advocates the use of it.

Multi Obstructive Expectation

Not content with just one sound argument for avoiding a proposal, the multi obstructive expector has developed his creative powers to such an extent that he can fabricate a multitude of limiting beliefs on a single theme. To him it is obvious that there are a thousand reasons for why it just won't work.

Awareness and the five levels

But these ways of doing life are not just restricted to one person. It is part of all our natures to access any of the five levels, and sometimes a blend of two different levels. Have you ever had those days when at one instant an idea seems like the best you have ever had, and the next minute you can't believe that you had once supported it? The

first stage of developing our powers of creative expectation is to become aware of our habitual reactions to the suggestions of others. Often we will leap into obstructive expectation when someone else comes up with an idea that we wish we had thought of, or worse still, better than the one we had put forward.

Spend time observing your initial internal reaction to the suggestions and thoughts of those around you. This practice will serve to make you more alert to the way you sabotage your own initiatives. For every Creative Expectation you have, you can rest assured that there will be a set of Multi Obstructive Expectations lurking in the wings to bring it down. Being vigilant can stop you destroying your most powerful dreams under a barrage of obstructive thoughts.

Creatively Expecting the Future

So what are the raw materials for building our expectations? And if Multi Creative Expectations are the most productive, how can we generate more of them?

To create vivid images of the future, we need to have the awareness of what it is exactly that we like and appreciate about the present? A golfer's focus is so intense on the picture of his desired outcome, that all else pales into insignificance. He doesn't see the trees, the water or the sand traps. He sees the flag vividly in his minds eye, but not before countless visits to real flags. He knows the shape, texture, weight, colour; the way the wind lifts and tosses it from side to side. He knows the importance of intimate knowledge of at least the essence or basic elements of his goal.

Similarly, a mountaineer sets his sights on the summit. His vision is shaped and moulded by thousands of images and memories of dozens of previous climbing trips. By piecing these experiences together into a picture of the moment he will become successful, he is actually surveying and pegging out the path that his road to success will follow. And this is more than just a mental picture. By visualising the event as he expects it to happen, physiologically his body reacts to his thoughts and he will actually experience a chemical high, triggered by this elaborate, dream-like state.

It is impossible to actively choose to create peace and calm in our lives without clearly being able to isolate and define those moments from our previous experiences. We need to be able to remember exactly what it felt, looked, tasted, smelled and sounded like on those previous occasions. How can we effectively create health, material wealth or relationships if we are constantly focussed on the aspects that didn't work last time?

Recall a moment when you felt really at peace with the world. Fully re-experience it. Now project that experience onto your screen of the future and extend the script to include a whole hour... day... week...

Picture a time when you achieved success. Fully experience every-thing that goes with this picture – how did it feel, who was there, what sounds and noises were surrounding you, what smells were in the air, what tastes were in your mouth, was your heart racing, were you breathing faster – and now overlay this image onto details of your future vision of success. At this point you are integrating the detailed memory of your past successful experience with the specifics of your goal, providing a vivid composite illustration of the moment of achievement.

An example might help. To use modern technological terms, it is a bit like digital enhancement of an old movie or even cutting and pasting from an old Word document into a new. Many successful sportsmen and women use this form of visualisation to improve their chances of success. If you have ever watched Olympic high jumpers you may have seen this process in action.

Waiting on the approach to the bar, the contestants can be observed as they mentally go through the motions of a successful jump. You can see their heads actually nodding as they re-trace their mental videos of hundreds of previously triumphant run-ups, leaps, landings and celebrations. They will *feel* their muscles working as they run, *feel* their bodies lift with the final thrust, experience the weightlessness as they float over the bar and begin falling towards the mat and re-live the elation as they acknowledge their own accomplishment as well as the roaring applause of 80 000 spectators. As a response to these exhilarating images the body administers its own 'performance enhancing drug' – most likely a mixture of adrenalin and endorphin – which acts as a sort of high-octane fuel boost for the actual attempt.

'Self observation is a tool for experiencing the present so that this information can then be moulded and shaped into a vivid and motivating vision for the future.'

Practising Creative Expectation

Just as we practice most endeavours, so too we can practice flexing our creative muscles. One of our favourites is *car parking spaces*. I'm not kidding! We constantly amuse our friends (our families are used to us by now) by reciting the Parking Mantra as we approach a shopping area or somewhere we need to leave the car. 'We always get a TPS' (top parking spot) repeated over and over while we cruise around the parking lot. Miraculously, we almost always get to park in the perfect spot; and even if we don't, the positive energy created by our optimism at least makes the search a pleasant experience.

Since I learnt the power of this process my life has been a continual chain of personal successes. I say *personal successes* because the things that I desire for myself may not be on your life shopping list, but my collection of mental trophies have continually whetted my appetite for the next challenge. One of my first conscious experiences of this phenomenon happened while attending a personal development workshop, many years ago in Australia, run by a psychiatrist named David Stratten.

Sixteen of us were seated on cushions in a circle in a magnificent rainforest retreat called the The Roundhouse. One by one and with David's guidance, we worked through our own individual life challenges. My burning issue at the time was my perceived inability to break out of the poverty trap I had been creating for myself and become well paid for doing work that I loved.

Eyes closed, I sat facing David and answered his questions about the sort of work I enjoyed and the type of environments that inspired, relaxed or excited me. Gradually a picture began to emerge of bush trails, streams, lakes, mountains and forests; and after only a few minutes, these pictures in my mind were almost real. I felt I could reach out and touch them. I could smell pine needles, hear the swishing of wind in high branches, see patches of dappled light on forest floors and taste the unmistakable flavour of water sipped from a mountain pool. I was there.

The questions on the type of work I enjoyed brought images of smiling happy faces, both small and large groups of people and a sense that I was somehow guiding them through some sort of life maze. The next phase was at once simple but incredibly powerful; so powerful in fact that even 15 years later, I can still vividly recall every minute detail of the scene. All he said was, 'Imagine there are two bubble-like structures before your eyes; one encapsulating the environmental image, and the other the image of you working. Now see the two bubbles merge into one.'

What emerged, almost immediately, was a vivid mental video clip of a stream, a rainforest, and a group of about fifteen people sitting around an open fire and listening intently while I spoke to them. It had all the elements of my ideal scene and to this day still has the power to simultaneously excite me and bring a smile of contentment. I was so pleased and motivated by the instant clarity of direction it gave me, I was willing to relinquish my control of the centre and return to my place in the circle. 'Before we finish,' said David, 'there's another aspect of this scenario we haven't covered yet.'

Returning me to the gathering in the forest, he asked me to imagine the sound of a vehicle approaching down a rough bush track between the trees. I described it as a white van with a sliding side door. As it pulled up about ten feet away, David asked me to picture myself greeting a man as he climbed out of the side door carrying a large leather satchel. Leaning down he unzipped the bag to reveal what looked to me like a fortune in rolled bank notes, stacked in several layers. It was the sort of thing you would expect to see as the proceeds of a robbery in an old movie.

And then came the challenge.

'Take what you think you are worth', he said. 'How much of this money do you think you should be paid for this job you have created?'

Silence. I stared back at him for what seemed like minutes. How much was I worth? He was challenging me to do something I had never seriously considered. I thought, 'You mean I have to put a figure on my financial value?' The image of me in the picture frame stood motionless for an age and then tentatively leaned down and scooped out two handfuls of notes from one corner of the top layer of bank notes. As I began to tell David what I had done I remember wishing I had had the courage to take more and at the same time being embarrassed at that thought – almost guilty for daring to believe that I was worth more.

In a blinding, life changing, flash of awareness I realised that the reason I had always found it difficult to create or accumulate large sums of money was that I didn't have a clear picture of it in my mind. I had always lived *down* to the limited image of success I had carried in my thoughts since childhood. For the most part I had experienced very few problems creating the things I desired in my life. Everything from homes and cars to relationships and travel had come to me with a speed and quality that was in direct proportion to the vibrance and clarity of the image I could hold of it. By many systems of reckoning I was deemed successful, but to earn more money than my father and brothers would have seemed like a form of betrayal – a breaking of the unwritten rules of parent and sibling rivalry.

'So, how much do you really deserve' he said.

With renewed zeal I pictured myself returning the two fistfuls of money to the carry bag. Wearing the sort of broad grin that accompanies such a startling revelation, I carefully re-zipped the bag, slipped my arm under the strap and strode off jauntily through the forest with my earned and deserved salary swinging casually from my shoulder. I knew from that moment on that my journey to wealth and its attendant financial security would be markedly easier.

Within four months I started work as a personal development facilitator at Camp Eden, which at that time was Australia's leading holistic health retreat, set in two hundred acres of rainforest near Queensland's Gold Coast. I was earning the highest salary I had ever received – for doing my ideal job! Coincidence? I don't think so. I have repeated the process so many times now that I have no doubt of its efficacy. It seems that the size and quality of my successes are only limited by the size and quality of my dreams. But... there is another crucial step.

A dream without a plan is just a wish

More often than not, once our vision is firmly set, the methods we need to convert it to reality will suddenly and magically appear. It is one of the amazing abilities of the subconscious to be able to work behind the scenes to devise a plan for the fulfilment of our imaginings. We are well advised to let it do the work for us. It is like we are standing at the counter of life and saying we need something; and, without prompting, the workroom at the back of the shop springs to life, the workers hell-bent on matching our purchase order.

Having waxed lyrical about the positive side of creative expectation, it is worth mentioning at this point that it is a perhaps unfortunate quirk of human nature that whatever can be used to create beneficial effects can also be used to create detrimental effects. And so it is with expectations. Creating drama or joy in our lives is all part of the same success<>disaster continuum – we generally get what we expect. In the next section we will discuss the relationship between success and stress and I will show that by using a simple and reasonably well known goal-setting framework, our creativity can be guided toward the success end of the spectrum.

Creating Success – an antidote to Stress?

I am stressed when I feel stuck; powerless; unable to control the mounting frustration; unable to make a difference. Small, regular successes give the accurate impression of progress. I am human. I was designed to move forward, to evolve, to learn by doing. It is imperative that I give myself every chance to appreciate my steps forward, no matter how small or tentative. One of the major keys to successful stress management is to adhere to the most basic principle of Goal Setting.

> *'It is of paramount importance that we learn to set our objectives just far enough out of reach to require effort and just close enough to ensure success.'*

If you have children, or know some, or at least remember being one at some time of your life, then you will probably relate to this. I remember watching my four-year-old son attempting to tie his own shoelaces for the first time. He had probably watched us tie them several hundred times. It looked easy enough. If these parent type people had accomplished such a trivial task in such a short space of time, how complicated could it be? But at that very first attempt... disaster. No stored experience of personal success on this particular task.

As a parent, watching my offspring struggle with any task brings a mixture of excitement and disappointment. The latter comes from an empathy born of involvement in similar personal learning experiences. The excitement stems from the knowledge of how the world actually works and an understanding that failure is never really failure, but a necessary step in the acquisition of knowledge. Self-knowledge. Possibly the most valuable knowledge we can gain.

So how as a parent do I seek to enhance instead of hinder this learning process?

> *'Learning is commendable.*
> *Understanding the process by which I learn,*
> *is invaluable.'*

Rather than expect the child to blindly challenge the task anew, I break it into small, bite-size chunks:

Chunk one: 'Right over left and under, then pull tight.' I guide, coach and applaud. I give credit for all the things he is doing well and has done well, and encouragement and direction for the parts he hasn't. Success! Chunk one mastered. And this is the most crucial phase of the whole story... we celebrate! This is the exact moment when we need to stop and engage in some heavy duty self indulgence. The endorphin hit from even a minute success gives us a boost that catapults us on to the next chunk. The small 'high' lubricates our creative and positive thinking channels. We are carried forward on a small wave of self belief.

As a climbing and abseiling instructor I've seen the look of achievement on countless faces. It is most obvious when the initial self belief of the student is quite low. Again, using a blend of instruction and encouragement, I guide them slowly down the cliff face, straightening them up when they wobble, picking them up if they fall; praising, directing and supporting. The moment their feet hit flat ground the smile on their face tells the story – they are ecstatic. But more than excitement at their own success, the look also says, 'I thought I couldn't do it, but have proved now that I can, so I wonder what else I am capable of?' This is the major benefit of allocating time to appreciate our wins; it pushes us on to the next challenge.

Anyway, back to my four-year-old. What does a little success do for his self-esteem? It soars! He has tackled a hitherto totally adult, albeit tiny, task and has attained a level of accomplishment that, in his eyes, surely sets him on the road to eventual mastery. He is ready to and, more importantly, enthusiastic about, tackling:

Chunk Two: Make a loop (a tree) with the lace on the right and hold it with your thumb and forefinger (the fat one and the pointing one)

Chunk Three: The left lace goes around the tree... etc.
Success, breeds success, breeds success...

It is such a simple model, yet the closer we get to our own perceived maturity, the faster we abandon the basic principles of learning. Everything we attach to our tree of knowledge has been acquired using a similar technique; try – fail – adjust – try – succeed – enjoy – try something new – fail... and yet as adults we become afraid to experiment. The failed experiments hang like warning bells around our necks, clanging when the reefs of failure lurk somewhere in the ocean ahead. Breaking our goals into smaller, more manageable pieces relieves some of the pressures that larger projects can invoke. This increases our chances of success as well as giving us more opportunities to celebrate at the milestones – and this in turn increases our chances for success.

> *'Whether you are four or forty-four, the principle is still the same – keep the longer vision in your heart and in your consciousness, but your focus on the next goal.'*

SMARTER Goal-setting

Monitoring progress towards our goals is of critical importance if we are to maintain momentum. Any tool or device we employ to achieve this aim should answer certain questions to be of practical use. Here are the questions I ask myself:

- What is the target?
- How far is it?
- How will I know when I have reached it?
  (and therefore when can I celebrate?)
- What are the measurable steps along the way where I can pat myself on the back for making progress?
- Can I do it?
- Do I want to do it?
- What's in it for me?
- Will I like doing it?

One of the most useful models for achieving regular and predictable successes is by making sure all your goal setting is SMARTER. 'Smarter than what?' you might say. Smarter than you would be if you set off without some sort of road map or structured plan!

SMARTER is an incredibly useful mnemonic and checklist for defining goals and keeping them on track. It stands for:

S	- Specific
M	- Measurable
A	- Achievable
R	- Realistic
T	- Time-bound
E	- Enjoyable
R	- Rewarding

Specific – Make certain that when you define your goal you specify every detail you can possibly think of. A clear and motivating vision of a future state is your most powerful ally in the process of creation. What would be your chances of scoring a goal without being able to see the goal posts; building a house without first drawing plans; or navigating through tricky waters without an accurate chart? Write the colour, shape, size, taste, sound of your goal. Identify how you want to feel when the result is achieved. Close your eyes and try to imagine the exact moment when you realise that you have succeeded

Measurable – Before breaking up the goal into measurable chunks, I suggest you go down to the 'T' in SMARTER to set a deadline for

34

successful completion. Quite simply, decide what is the date you want to see, feel, experience your success. Once you have this firmly set, begin the process of deciding each individual step along the way. Measurable steps must be quantifiable in terms of time, or amount, or number, so that it is obvious to *you* that you have made progress. They could be: number of sales; confirmation that your holiday has been booked; a certain amount of money in a savings account; a positive work appraisal. They can in fact be anything that you can hold up and say, 'Yes. This means I am on track toward reaching my ultimate goal.'

Your first step could be to set aside an hour to write down your SMARTER goal in detail. Start with the first thing you need to do. How will you know you have done it and how will you celebrate completion of this step? Then systematically go through and identify any point along the route where you can justifiably stop for a moment and pat yourself on the back.

Achievable – This is a tricky one. On a day when your negative thoughts are proliferating at an exponential rate, there are very few scenarios you will see as achievable. Try to keep an objective outlook. It sometimes helps to ask whether or not you think someone else would be able to achieve this particular target. If the answer is yes, then it is probably the current state of your self-esteem that is the problem. Even if in the back of your mind you are thinking, 'Yes, it is achievable, but only by Superman or Wonderwoman', mark it down as a 'Yes'. Tomorrow you will probably be feeling more positive and may even want to increase the size of the challenge! If, on the other hand, you don't believe it is achievable by anyone, re-adjust your goal, or the measurable step, to something more feasible. In other words – always set yourself up for a win.

Realistic – There is often confusion between the two terms, Realistic and Achievable. A short example may highlight the difference. It would be achievable to build a bridge across the English Channel between Dover and Calais. We have the technology and the materials and the engineering capabilities to achieve this, and we may even be able to construct it in an incredibly short timescale if we employed thousands of people and allocated huge amounts of our resources; but is it realistic? Just because something is desirable doesn't mean we should have a realistic expectation regarding its completion. This aspect of the checklist can also be flavoured by our moods or the current state of our self-esteem. Again, remain as objective as possible when assessing the realistic-ness (is that a word?) of your goal.

Time-bound – I prefer to use the term *time-bound* rather than timely or time specific, as it implies that I will be bound, almost by an inferred contract with myself, to deliver on the prescribed date. I am creating a self-imposed deadline. As I mentioned under *Measurable*, it is important to incorporate this check at the same time as stating the specifications of the goal. Whether the goal or the measurable steps are *achievable* or *realistic* will depend on how much time I have allotted to the tasks required for successful completion.

Enjoyable – As with anything we attempt in life, it makes sense that we will probably become more motivated and try harder if we find the whole event a pleasurable experience. Sometimes this is not so easy, but I'm sure if you look deep enough into any task, there will be something to give you a laugh. It may be linked to the next phase of the checklist – is it rewarding?

Rewarding – I will probably create some dissension here, but I firmly believe that we are all a lot more intrinsically motivated than we might like to admit. The WIIFM factor (What's in it for me?) plays a huge role in our decision-making. I certainly enjoy helping other people, and I have been in helping or caring professions most of my life, but do I do it solely for *them*, or do I do it because I enjoy the feeling it gives me to help *them*? A debatable point. Whether it is a material, financial or emotional reward is largely irrelevant, but I am likely to be far more motivated if there is to be a perceived personal gain of some type.

*'Stretch just far enough to increase your enthusiasm,
not your stress levels.'*

Real Success and our modern version of *stress* find it extremely difficult to co-exist in the same person. Of course you can probably challenge me with lists of people you see as both successful and stressed, and my retort would be that real success is measured in means other than purely financial or material. No doubt these are important, but they will create a more complete and sustainable success when combined with personal growth in the four major aspects of our lives – Physical, Mental, Emotional and Spiritual (See chapter on Lifestyle Matters)

Creating Success using Enlightened Responses

So how does awareness and the Enlightened Response fit into my SMARTER goal-setting plan? I need to be aware of my own capabilities, my fears, strengths, weaknesses, and also aware of the environment in which I will be working to achieve my goal. I need to be able to accurately observe and identify which particular aspects of the goal are the ones that I truly desire. Creating a vision of a successful outcome will require that I imagine and visualise in detail each aspect of the steps toward the goal and the final result itself. I also need to be aware of my reactions to any hurdles I may encounter along the way. With awareness of my habitual reactions I can use my PAUSE button to allow me enough time to choose an Enlightened Response instead of rolling along the easier road of my entrenched behaviour patterns.

- **Stop**
- **Observe**
- **Ascertain the reality of the situation**
- **Choose an appropriate response**

And I'd like to complete this section with a quote.

> *'Communicate candidly, face reality*
> *and control your own destiny.'*

JACK WELCH, CEO of General Electric from 1981-2001, attributes his success to these three concepts taught to him by his mother when he was a child. As one of the most successful entrepreneurial business achievers of the last 100 years, does Jack Welch (and his mother) have something to say to us about setting our targets?

In a way, the first two of these pieces of advice are about the past and the present and the third is about the future. And isn't that what goal-setting is all about. The way we EVALUATE past and present EVENTS provides the basis by which we formulate our EXPECTATION (objective/vision/goal) for the future. Could it be that the pathway to success in business is the very same as the pathway to success in relationships... or sport... or life?

Setting SMARTER goals could increase your measurable successes... immeasurably!

And in <u>YOUR</u> life...

1. Which of the childhood 'I want' methods do you often use as an adult. For example, do you still resort to sulking to get your own way, or throw the occasional tantrum?

2. Do you tend to use one level of expectation more than the others? e.g. Always see the problems (Multi Obstructive), or conversely, only see the benefits? (Multi Creative)

3. Can you create a vivid mental screenplay of the future you want?

4. In which areas of your life do you need to create more success so that you feel less stressed?

5. Using the SMARTER framework, set out a plan for achieving at least one of your goals. No, not tomorrow – NOW!

6. Create a 'Treasure Map' to help motivate you toward your goals. Simply cut out pictures and words describing things that you desire and that motivate you from old magazines, travel brochures and advertising pamphlets etc, and glue them on to a large piece of coloured card. Stick it up in a prominent position in your house where you will see it often. (mine usually go behind the toilet door!) It will serve as a reminder of your goals and you can check your progress regularly by identifying which objectives you have reached and which still need some work. It will fine-tune your internal focus mechanism known as your RAS. (More on this in Chapter 12 – *Personality*)

THE CREATIVE POWER OF EXPECTATION

IN THIRTY WORDS OR LESS...

'Our creative expectations systematically devise a road map for us to follow to accomplish both simple chores and lifetime goals. Success or stress – the choice is ours.'

*'Understanding
is only a perception
and bears little
resemblance to reality.'*

CHAPTER FOUR

THE EVENT

Facts v Perceptions

We spend a seemingly inordinate amount of time establishing full awareness of the 'facts' before making decisions. What are these facts and where do they reside? Can I make do with my perceptions until they show up?

The only information we know about the present situation is the parts that we are aware of. And even these parts are *as we see them*, not necessarily *the way they are*. When someone asks me where I live I could quite honestly answer, 'Relative to what?' All my awarenesses (many individual moments of awareness) of where I am, are based on relative comparisons to the positions of other objects. For example, if I say I live in No.24, the next question is, 'On which street?' 'Smith street.' Great. 'In which suburb?' 'Highgate.' 'Is that London or Brisbane?' ...and so on. The next obvious questions are, 'Which country', then 'Which continent', and in the not too distant future, 'Which planet... solar system... galaxy?'

All my life I've been aware of a pair of stars in the southern sky called The Pointers and how to use them to find The Southern Cross. I've also *known* that the brighter of the two Pointers was called Alpha Centauri. It wasn't until I got the chance to examine this particular star through a sixteen-inch telescope that I discovered that it is actually three stars, not one as I had previously thought. It won't hurt here to repeat the old adage:

'Things aren't always what they seem'

As part of my general *answer a few trivial pursuit questions* knowledge, I've always had the figure of 'Four and a half light-years' as my answer to the question; 'How far away is our closest stellar neighbour, Alpha Centauri?' The part of me that always wants to understand everything was completely humbled by the revelation that the distance between two of the three stars, which we see as one star called Alpha Centauri, is approximately thirteen thousand times the distance between Earth and our Sun.

Even this little mind-blower paled into insignificance when I learned that our sun and Alpha Centauri are only two of some three hundred thousand million stars in our galaxy we call the Milky Way... and there are millions of galaxies! And just how big is the Milky Way? Well it takes light about one hundred thousand years to cross from one side to the other at a speed of approximately three hundred thousand kilometres per second! Make sure you pack a sandwich to eat on the journey, and I won't wait up for you! In the past when people have asked me, 'What do you know?' I never realised how truthful I was being when I answered, 'Not much.'

How much do I really know compared to how much I think I know?

I've seen this conundrum illustrated as a graph called the Knowledge Pie Chart.

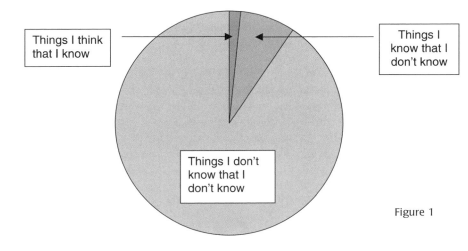

Figure 1

The circle represents everything there is to know

Things we think we know

I have purposely made this a very small segment, but still theorise that I may have grossly exaggerated it. By virtue of the fact that I am continually learning new things, and have been throughout my life, I have to conclude that there are still many things to know. The size of this section will vary slightly from person to person, but not noticeably. Items in this segment can include things like; how to tie my shoelaces, the recipe for pumpkin scones, who won last years Grand National and my six times table.

Things I know that I don't know

The things I know that I don't know include: How to fly a plane, the recipe for Crepe Suzette, who won the 1928 Melbourne Cup and the mathematical formula for calculating the trajectory for a Space Shuttle landing. I also know that I don't know (but sometimes I forget that I don't know) how the world looks through the eyes of another human being. I don't have their exact genetic, physical, mental, emotional, psychological or social attributes or abilities, and I certainly can't match their life experiences and especially the way they perceived those experiences. So why do I go through life expecting that the world *should* see things the way I do? And why do I get annoyed when it doesn't? I'll discuss this further in the chapter on Personality.

Things I don't know that I don't know

By far the biggest portion of this graph represents the millions of things that I have no idea that it is possible to know. For example, I only recently discovered that there are different coloured stars in the universe. Before discussing this with an astronomer, I was completely unaware of this *fact* (if such a thing exists). My best friend's seventeen year old son, Kris, theorises that the ancient pyramids of Egypt are merely an example of intergalactic graffiti left by visiting aliens. And who's to say he's wrong?

As human beings we have an intense desire to know, or at least appear to others as if we know the facts. The truth is, even the things we think we know – and again, I think I've been very generous with the size of this sector – are probably inaccurate in many cases.

So… please don't allow me to convince you that I understand anything. – past, present or future. The best any of us can hope to do is

observe and be aware of what we think is going on around us. Maybe we can never be sure of our facts, only our perceptions, or are they merely *illusions?*

> *'Understanding is only a perception and bears little resemblance to reality.'*

Perception

> *'If the doors of perception were cleansed, everything would appear to man as it is. Infinite. For man has closed himself up, till he sees all things through narrow chinks of his cavern.'*
> **WILLIAM BLAKE**

Our thinking can create walls of fear through which we timidly observe the world. If thinking can build them, then just as surely it can tear them down.

Perception: 'Interpreting the information we receive through our sensory organs or the process by which we make sense of our sensations.'
FROM 'PSYCHOLOGY – AN INTRODUCTION'

We often can't change the event, but we can change our perceptions of the event. When we train our minds to perceive things differently, our bodies will react accordingly.

For example, if I'm planning a trip to the beach and wake to find a cold, rainy day, my mind will probably judge this as 'bad'. This thought is immediately channelled to my Hormone Distribution System which supplies a dose of *downer* to match my negative thought. Conversely, a sunny morning will instantly trigger an endorphin rush and a mild case of euphoria will ensue, unless of course I have other negative thoughts influencing the system, which cancel out my positive thought. In my experience, one perceived broken heart is worth about ten sunny days – such is the plight of a romantic.

The mistakes I make can be viewed as setbacks or sounding boards – if I'm making progress it means that I am moving. As a human being, as long as I keep moving, there will be times when things just don't work out the way I planned. I can choose to perceive these as failures and give my system a chemical beating, or I can choose to see it all as part of the scheme of things and an indication that I have succeeded in staying on course. At that point I can smile at my own good fortune and administer another hit of *feel good*.

I remember being absolutely distraught at missing a train when I was desperately trying to get out of New Delhi a few years ago. An hour later I climbed aboard an express to Shimla in the Himalayan foothills. Within another two hours my express had passed the train I had missed as it lay in a siding with engine failure. One way or another the events of my life will either present me with a win or a lesson… and isn't that a win?

So…how do I gain control of this seemingly automatic reaction? How do I teach my mind to accept rather than judge, to go with the flow instead of damming the tide?

Respond v React

The answers to the preceding questions lay in my ability to become aware of that split second, immediately after one or more of my senses has received a message, when I have time to either choose an appropriate response or allow my automatic reaction to take over.

Below are extracts from the Australian Concise Oxford Dictionary definitions of the words: React, Reaction, Respond and Response.

React

3. 'Make counter-attack.'
4. 'be actuated by repulsion against,
   tend in reverse or backward direction.'

Reaction

1 '…immediate or first impression; tendency to
   oppose change or to return to former system.'

Notice how these first two imply *habit* and *rebellion*, contrasting with the next two, which lean toward *choice* and *flow*.

Respond

> 2. 'Show sensitiveness to by behaviour or change.'

Response

> 1. '...action, feeling, movement, change etc.
> elicited by stimulus or influence.'

Conclusion:

> To react seems to imply a move against change and respond a move toward change. What if I could choose to 'respond to' the events of my life, not 'react against' them? Would that improve my quality of life and reduce my stress?

Developing awareness is a skill that can be learned

When I am not truly aware of the reality in any given event, I can bounce through life like those silver balls in a pin-ball machine. I am constantly buffeted by those events, sights, sounds, opinions and even my own self-indulgent view of life – the world according to me. And unfortunately, the filter through which I see my world is different to everyone else's, and consequently my expectations and judgements have their own unique colours and flavours. Expecting that other people will see the world the way I do is like expecting that a Volkswagen will do 150mph merely because it was designed by the same people who created the Porsche. I need to be able to gain objectivity. I need to understand that your reality is often very different to my reality and that your view is merely different, not wrong. If I can stand back, observe, and see *what is* rather than *what I think it is*, I will have a much firmer grip on the steering wheel of my life.

And in <u>YOUR</u> life...

1. Start making a list of what you really know, compared to what you think you know. You will probably find that the first list is incredibly short. For example: Do you know the colour of an apple? How your heart works? Why the moon is white?

2. Do you really understand the way you think and feel? No? Then do you sometimes expect that others should?

3. Do you really know the way others think and feel? Do you sometimes expect that you should?

4. Do you sometimes act on perceptions rather than facts?

5. How many events do you react to, instead of choosing to respond? If your perception is that you don't have time to choose a response, you may want to think about changing that perception.

6. Remember the last time you had a major 'knee-jerk' reaction to an event. What was the expectation that was mismatched with the event? Could you have changed the expectation or the event or the evaluation? Faced with the same situation again, what, if anything, would you choose to do differently? What would be an Enlightened Response?

THE EVENT
IN THIRTY WORDS OR LESS...

'Learning to tell the difference
between facts and perceptions
will help us to choose
Enlightened Responses
instead of habitual reactions.'

*'If you find yourself needing
to judge something
'Right' or 'Wrong', 'Good' or 'Bad',
then stop and ask yourself
why. Will judging help
you solve the problem?'*

CHAPTER FIVE

THE EVALUATION

'Our lives are ruled by expectation and judgement'

Time and time again I am being reminded of the accuracy of this statement. *Expectation* before an event and *judgement* of the results after it, form the very core of my belief about my life. If a particular situation turns out different to the mental picture I had of it, then my judgement mechanism cranks up to place the event somewhere on a continuum between celebration and despair. Following rapidly behind this judgement is a closely matching chemical (hormonal) hit which produces a *feeling*.

Expectations and judgements are merely thoughts. Perhaps these thoughts are the root of all my problems. But then again, maybe it's not the actual thought that causes me problems, but the way I evaluate that thought.

Thought Evaluation System

The Thought Evaluation process begins with an expectation based on our memories of past events and more particularly, how we evaluated those events. Let's start with an example and follow it as it passes through the Thought Evaluation System. (Figure 2)

Even though I may have seen thousands of grey, wet days, something in my brain wants me to believe that tomorrow will be clear and sunny. I have planned a picnic with my girlfriend and the imagined pictures in my head are coated with the sugary sweetness of expectation.

I rise at eight in the morning and my senses are awakened to thunderstorms and howling winds. The messages from my eyes (seeing the wet roads) ears (hearing the rain beating on to the roof), nose (which can smell the dampness) and the built-in thermometer of my skin (which feels the coolness in the air); all tell me that it is not a good day for the *event* (the picnic). There is a mismatch with my *expectation*. The TES judges this to be a bad thing and fires the appropriate signal down the line to the negative end of the evaluation scale.

THOUGHT EVALUATION SYSTEM

EVENT
SEE
HEAR
SMELL
TASTE
FEEL
THROUGH
PERCEPTION
FILTER
Event collides
with
EXPECTATION

GOOD   NEUTRAL   BAD
EVALUATION

LOVE   REALLY LIKE   LIKE   DISLIKE REALLY DISLIKE HATE

FEEL GOOD CHEMICALS   PHYSICAL REACTION   FEEL BAD CHEMICALS

EUPHORIC   HAPPY   AMUSED   IRRITATED   ANNOYED   ANGRY

Figure 2

Judgement and our chemical factory

The body's chemical reaction is that the hypothalamus, pituitary gland and adrenal glands all link up to issue a hormonal response to these electrical impulses. In the case of the *bad day* scenario, the physical responses to these hormone cocktails can be anything from depression to teeth clenching to wall punching. Of course the sunny *good day* chain of thoughts would most probably end with an endorphin rush producing smiles and enthusiasm.

If you find yourself needing to judge something 'Right' or 'Wrong', 'Good' or 'Bad', then stop and ask yourself why. Will judging help you solve the problem? If this problem involves another person, will judging enhance your relationship with them? Will it enhance communication if the other party 'feels' judged? If it is not solving the problem then maybe it is part of the problem.

The Enlightened Response technique

Left to their own devices our thoughts will often feel a need to classify and evaluate themselves either positive or negative, bounce back and forth, comparing themselves with the past and postulating about the future, and cap it off with an habitual reaction. Practising Self Observation will teach us to be more objective, increase our awareness and enable us to stand back momentarily and make *enlightened* decisions. i.e. decisions made with a clearer understanding of the way our thought processes work. The resultant responses are more likely to be ones we have chosen, not those forced upon us by routine or custom.

Our habitual reactions have become firmly entrenched through years of following the same, well-worn path. For us to be able to influence this well established system and redirect it, will take practice and perseverance. Our minds will want to keep on thinking the way they always have — unencumbered. But the rewards for persisting will far outweigh any inconvenience initially encountered. Hang in there! It will be worth it.

And in <u>YOUR</u> life...

1. Make a list of the different feelings you have had in the last couple of hours. If you are anything like me, you probably felt happy and smiled about something; and then within an instant, you probably felt a little anxious; and something might have made you a little angry or at least irritated. Now try to trace each of these occurrences back to the thought that triggered it. What was the thought that made you smile? What did you think to make you feel fearful or anxious? Was there an event that you judged as 'bad' that triggered a shot of adrenalin to make you fell angry, your face frown and your heart start thumping?

2. Have you noticed anybody who exhibited a behaviour that indicated that they were feeling something? What was your perception of their feelings? Take a guess at what the thought was that triggered their feelings. Now here's a tricky part. What did you feel as you observed their behaviour? What was the thought that triggered that feeling? Did you judge their behaviour and/or their feelings as 'good' or 'bad'?

51

I'm not suggesting that you spend all day going through this process, but a few minutes really studying these events will raise your awareness to the *fact* that you are merely reacting to your perceptions. Change your perceptions, choose your responses and change your life.

THE EVALUATION

IN THIRTY WORDS OR LESS...

'Evaluating an event as either good or bad will trigger a chemical hit that we experience as a feeling. So... if we judge it as good, we'll feel good.'

CHAPTER SIX

AWARENESS

Awareness is the key to just about anything we want or need to do. It is the starting point for all our endeavours from trivial tasks to major projects. Before we can figure out where we are going, we must be aware of where we are. Without awareness of where we are we have no starting point for calculating how to get where we want to go. And that's fine if we're not planning to go anywhere, but most of us have at least one major project to complete before we move on to our next life – whatever form that may take.

What if I were to find out half way through a journey that the place I was heading for is actually the place I used to be? I need to be honest with myself about what I am feeling if I am to have any chance of changing how I feel. And if I am to adjust my attitude I need to be aware of the way I think and often it also helps to be aware of how I came to think that way, although this is not imperative. If I waited until I understood everything before I took action, I'd probably never take action.

Question: 'And how do I develop Awareness?

Answer: 'By observing my life instead of being caught up in the turmoil of it. And the best way I know of doing this is by practising some form of Mind Management or Observation.

There are literally thousands of methods and techniques for teaching your mind to focus on what you want it to instead of it following its own agenda. In Chapter 8 I have included fifty different scripts for you to follow which will give you a feel for the basic skills required. And don't panic. If it wasn't simple I wouldn't be able to use it myself, never mind write a book about it!

And what if THINKING and MIND MANAGEMENT held the answer to that most burning of questions: 'What is the Meaning of life?'

The only meaning life has is the meaning we choose to give it.
Life only exists for us in our thinking.
We think about what has happened.
We think about what is happening.
We think about what will happen.
If we manage our thinking, we manage our lives.

But don't just take my word for it. What do the greatest minds, cultures, philosophers and religions say about thinking and its extended derivative – philosophy?

Famous Quotes on Thinking

The following is a list of major historical players thinkers, theologians and gurus who all, in one form or another, seem to agree that:

'Our thoughts govern our lives. Therefore we can change our lives by simply changing our thoughts.'

In many cases I have added a brief authors perspective.

~·~

The Mind is a gift. It helps us to process and understand the world around us.
LOUIS FARMER, ONONDAGA AMERICAN INDIAN ELDER

Without our mind, and therefore our thinking, there is no world to perceive, understand or of which to have views and opinions.

~·~

Whether I think I can or I can't, I'm probably right!
HENRY FORD

It is commonly held that 'Thoughts lead to belief's, beliefs lead to actions, actions lead to results.' Doesn't it then make sense that positive thoughts will eventually produce positive results?

~·~

We are what we think. All that we are arises with our thoughts. With our thoughts, we make the world.
BUDDHA

And in the next quote the famous philosopher Voltaire echoed with:

~·~

I think, therefore I am.
VOLTAIRE

The eternal conundrum. The common argument is that even though a rock doesn't think (Does it?) surely it still physically exists? I believe the key here is that thinking makes the rock exist for me, and without my past memories, my present perceptions or my future imaginings of it, in my consciousness it truly does not exist.

∽∽

Understanding the nature and process of thought is paramount if we are to manage our thinking. The source of all our pain is our thinking. The source of all negative emotion is negative thought. All that we are is the result of what we have thought; it is founded on our thoughts; it is made up of our thoughts. We tend to think that our enemies are without. The truth is they are mostly within.
DALAI LAMA
DURING HIS TEACHINGS AT DHARAMSALA. MARCH 1998

Which seems to fit very nicely with something that Mahatma Ghandi said.

∽∽

The only devils in the world are the ones found in our own hearts and minds.
MAHATMA GANDHI

Which begs the question: Does evil really exist as a separate entity, or is it purely a product of the mind?

∽∽

The true path is only difficult for those who make distinctions. Do not like, do not dislike. Then everything will become clear
MASTER SENG TS'AN.

Our judgement is a product of our internal thought processes. Is then something only good or bad if I decide it to be?

∽∽

Things only have the value that I give them. Things or relationships don't contain happiness. If chocolate contained happiness it would make us happy every time we ate it.
TUBDEN CHODREN

∽∽

The true man of ancient times knew nothing of loving life, knew nothing of hating death. He received something and took pleasure in it; he forgot about it and handed it back again.
CHUANG TZU

How much more could we enjoy our lives if we just stopped dissecting it and merely appreciated it?

∽∽

The only difference between a weed
and a flower is the Judgement
SAI BABA

∾∾

There is only one thing a philosopher can be relied upon
to do, and that is to contradict other philosophers.
WILLIAM JAMES

We are all philosophers, each of us having our own unique views and opinions of the strange workings of the world and it's inhabitants.

∾∾

If your philosophy doesn't grow corn, find a new philosophy.
OLD AMERICAN INDIAN PROVERB

Thinking leads to philosophy; philosophy is the breeding ground for results. If the results you get aren't the ones you want, go back to the start and look at your thinking.

∾∾

In philosophy we must distrust the things we understand
too easily, as well as the things we don't understand.
VOLTAIRE

Don't we just fool ourselves into thinking that we understand anything at all? Understanding is only a perception and bears little resemblance to reality.

∾∾

If the doors of perception were cleansed, everything
would appear to man as it is. Infinite. For man has
closed himself up, till he sees all things
through narrow chinks of his cavern.
WILLIAM BLAKE

Our thinking can create walls of fear through which we timidly observe the world. If thinking can build them, then just as surely it can tear them down.

∾∾

The highest possible stage in moral culture is when
we recognise that we ought to control our thoughts.
CHARLES DARWIN

Surely acting on every single thought we have would bring about disaster for most of us. Accepting that we need to manage our thought processes is the first major step in successfully managing our lives.

∾∾

*Every philosopher can be assured that his own system
rest on no surer foundations than the rest.*
ROUSSEAU

Another way of putting this is: The only person who has it all
together is the person who knows that no-one has it all together.

∽∽

*In the realms of the unconscious mental life
there is no such thing as exhaustion.*
C.G CARUS

Even when our bodies sleep, our thoughts are still active.

∽∽

*Imagination depends mainly upon memory, but there is
a small percentage of creating something out of nothing with it.
We can invent a trifle more than can be got at by mere
combination of remembered thing*s.
SAMUEL BUTLER (1912)

Memories are merely stored thoughts. What we construct from them
is up to us.

∽∽

What is now proved was once only imagined.
WILLIAM BLAKE (1790)

All aspects of creativity start and finish with a thought.

∽∽

*Many have original minds who do not think it.
They are led away by custom.*
KEATS (1818)

How many times have you had a brilliant idea, or at least what you
think is a good one, and have shelved it at the first sign of disagree-
ment or criticism? (Attacked by the hounds of custom)

∽∽

*Who decides whether you shall be happy
or unhappy? The answer – YOU DO!*
NORMAN VINCENT PEALE
(From 'The Power of Positive Thinking' – 1953)

It is widely accepted that we can change our thoughts. And if happiness and sadness are not the result of thoughts, then what are they?

∽∽

Emotion Follows Thought
ROBERT RAZZ

It has been said that Emotion is just 'Energy (E) in Motion'. But what sets it in motion if not a thought?

∽∾

If you want to be peaceful, do it inside
and stop putting the blame on the world.
ROBERT RAZZ

We make the world and the weather and other people responsible for our stress. But have you ever noticed that when we point the finger of blame, there are actually another three fingers pointing back at us. It would seem a fair indication of where the blame lies!

∽∾

We argue against reality.
Do you know of anything more futile?
ROBERT RAZZ

We like to say 'Look at the way the world is and look at the way those people behave. It shouldn't be like that!' Reality dictates that it 'is' like that. How long are we going to fight for peace instead of just being peaceful? We only argue if we think or judge something to be different to what we expected. Perhaps if we didn't judge it, we wouldn't need to argue against it.

∽∾

Nothing is either good or bad,
except that thinking makes it so.
WILLIAM SHAKESPEARE

Our thinking is shaped by our experiences. Different experiences of the same event, requires different thinking. Not good or bad, just different.

∽∾

In the second of the original Star Wars trilogy, Luke Skywalker is training to become a Jedi Knight when Yoda orders him to enter a dark, eerie cavern from which strange threatening sounds are emanating. 'What's in there?' he inquires fearfully. 'Only what you take with you', replies the wise old Jedi master.

Unless we challenge the fearful thoughts in our minds they will always travel with us.

∽∾

There are as many opinions as there are people;
each has his own point of view.
TERENCE (190 – 159 BC)

We had better get used to the fact that no-one else's thoughts will ever exactly match our own.

∾∾

I've travelled all over the world
and all I've managed to do is come home.
MAHATMA (GREAT SOUL) GANDHI

Another version of 'the grass is always greener...' syndrome. Wherever we go and whatever we do, the true meaning of who we are will be always carried with us in our thoughts.

∾∾

I'm going to give my all to winning but I'm not
going to define myself by the result.
JONATHAN EDWARDS,
WORLD AND OLYMPIC TRIPLE JUMP CHAMPION

The results I create are only part of the definition of who I really am. As part of my humanness I will have results that will be varied in their measurable value, including their quality, effectiveness and their impact on others. Will every new result define a new me? No, I am who I think I am and the results I produce from those thoughts are only part of what I do.

∾∾

Faith lights one step ahead in the darkness
TOM ROBINSON,
SINGER/SONGWRITER

And what is faith if not a vision and a feeling and thoughts and beliefs about the future. Faith in God, spirit, mankind, self – all these will lift us up and carry us forward.

Mind Management

The previous section elaborated on numerous thoughts on thinking. If I am to believe these celebrated thinkers, then how can I learn to take control of *my* thoughts and therefore *my* life?

The following pages contain a set of basic ideas that can be used as they are to improve mind management or they can be developed or modified to suit your needs. You will notice that I use the term *mind*

management as opposed to *mind control*. To my way of thinking the word control implies that an element of force is required, whereas the term I would use would be something like **assertive persuasion**. If my mind 'wanders off' in one of these exercises (and it will) the part of my consciousness assigned to keep my thoughts on track will end up in a bitter struggle if it tries to instigate a wrestling match with the part that wanders. Exactly the same dynamic can be seen in my inter-actions with other people. Confronted with another person trying to force me to do anything, my first reaction is usually to dig my heels in. If on the other hand they approach me with tact, confidence and a solid argument, I am much more likely to follow their directions. My mind is no different. The voices in my head are much like my friends – they respond to reason faster than they will to coercion.

So how do I keep my mind from wandering?

I asked this of a friend who had been a Tibetan Buddhist monk for twenty years.

'Describe to me what happens when you meditate' he said.

'Well, I go along OK for a while and then my mind just seems to get bored and races off to think about something more interesting or I start worrying about a certain problem in my life'.

'You too?' was his surprising reply. And then he said 'What do you do about it?'

I told him that I usually coax it back on to the breath or whatever it is I'm choosing to focus on. 'But it gets so tiring and monotonous!' I added.

'And that's the point where we often give up', he said, 'and the mind wins a battle to become our master instead of our employee.'

The mind has the power to withdraw energy for anything it decides is not stimulating or exciting. The same thing happens in our daily work when we are confronted with a task we've labelled 'boring'. The brain shuts down the organs and glands that distribute the chemicals which in turn give us that burst of energy we need to complete the task. When our mind is racing from thought to thought there is no clear message as to where the energy is needed, so it refuses to supply any. We feel sluggish and stuck.

Success comes when we patiently and continually lead our thoughts back to where we want them and eventually the mind tires in the face of our dogged persistence. Our thoughts become clearer and less confused, our ability to focus improves and our energy levels rise to match the task we have focussed on. A wandering mind is not a sign of failure but an indication of humanness. The only failure is in not trying in the first place. Just as in life, success is synonymous with consistent effort, not merely positive results.

In other words:

> **'Rejoice in the knowledge that you are playing the game, not in the number of points on the scoreboard.'**

The positive effects of self observation are not only an end in themselves, even though these alone are reason enough for practising. The lessons learned from daily practise of mind management techniques overflow into every corner of our lives producing clearer patterns of thought, an improved ability to focus and higher levels of energy for the tasks we choose to tackle.

The quality of my life is governed not by what happens, but how I perceive what happens. Therefore, if I can manage my perceptions (the way I think) then I can effectively manage my life.

There are mountains of both anecdotal and scientific evidence to suggest that self observation is, and has been throughout history, the most effective method for improving mind management. And it's much cheaper than valium.

There is very little stress in the present moment

To relate this statement to something I mentioned earlier, most of the mental activity which causes my stress is about the expectations I have before an event and the seemingly endless evaluations I embark on after the event, but very little about the event itself. My expectations are based on my vast collection of personal, past experiences of events, added to the events I've been told about, heard about, read about or seen on TV, movies or video; and then multiplied by the power of my imagination. What a potent cocktail!

On one of my study tours to India, I spent some time at the Parma

Niketan ashram in the Northern Indian town of Rishikesh. This vibrant town on the upper reaches of the Ganges became famous in the late 1960's as a Mecca for westerners seeking spiritual enlightenment. I was a slow starter and didn't arrive there until almost thirty years later, but my goals were not dissimilar to my predecessors on the hippy trail all those years ago.

Included in the meagre tariff were daily yoga and meditation classes and an array of health treatments which included massages and steam baths. The pathway leading from the accommodation block to the health centre was lined with a wonderful assortment of tall rose bushes and cut through the middle of a vast garden. Following the first Yoga session, I was wandering back through the avenue of thorny stems and huge red, yellow and pink flowers, when one particularly beautiful deep pink rose fought for my attention above all the others. I guess in a way, it spoke to me. The message was something along the lines of:

'Stop and appreciate me now, for tomorrow I may have changed.'

It certainly wasn't a new message. The saying 'Stop and smell the roses' has probably been around as long as the species itself, and it has surfaced in songs, poetry and prose numerous times. But this rose spoke to me, and me alone. It was pointed and unambiguous; the effect both instant and profound. Without exaggeration, this single and outwardly trivial event continues to influence every facet of my life. The picture of this rose, which would seem to be etched indelibly on both my conscious and subconscious mind, reminds me that within every thought, and every event on any given day there lies the seeds of a lesson. Merely being aware of the presence of these lessons will allow my tree of self-knowledge to sprout another branch.

If creating peace in my life is a by-product of being aware of my progress, then finding *instant peace* is as simple as seeking out the rose in the tangled garden of every moment. When I drift off course and find myself trapped in the back-forth, past-future, memories-fears cycle of stress, the rose can serve as my anchor to the present. Whatever my garden of the present looks like, if I take the time to observe the whole scene carefully, to search among the weeds and tangles of thorny vines and spider webs, I will gain perspective on the large and small events of my life, acknowledge my successes and find the rose of peace.

My Rishikesh Rose still 'speaks to me', reminding me how much peace there can be in the present. Rishikesh, India, 1998.

'Somewhere in the tangled garden of the
present, there blooms a rose
Sometime in this complicated tale of ife,
I'll find some reason
When futures cease to tempt and pasts
no longer rule and haunt my days
Then I will see the colours of the spring,
no matter what the season

I am here, the time is now
There's never been a finer hour
A part of me always knows
Thorns are just a pathway to the rose'

From the song 'PATHWAY TO THE ROSE' © Ross Page 1999

So… if awareness of life's continual lessons is the key to planning my next steps, then how do I make that key?

The raw materials are the thousands of daily experiences I encounter and self-observation is the cast that shapes them into usable moments of awareness. The principles of creating awareness through self-observation are exactly the same for assessing the subtleties of my personal beliefs as they are for noticing a change in the weather. Collecting these snapshots of my individual views of the world and filing them for future reference will provide a personal library of knowledge from which I can forge my expectations for the future. These awarenesses are the building blocks of success, however I gauge it.

'We stress ourselves more about what has happened
and what might happen than what is happening.'

And in <u>YOUR</u> life…

1. We are all philosophers – you, me and anyone who thinks. Every time you think or say something wise, write it down. Looking back on these gems of enlightened thought does great things for your self belief.

2. On a scale of 1 to 10, where do you rate yourself as a philosopher? Do you see yourself as a thinker? Why should your thoughts be any less valuable than someone else's? The fact that you can see the wisdom in the words of others means that you must already have similar thoughts in your own head. This results in you agreeing with the philosopher.

3. Just as a test to see how well you can focus your mind, spend a couple of minutes looking at your watch or a clock with a second hand. Digital will do just fine. Start with a new minute and time how long you can focus only on the clock face before your mind wanders off to do its own thing.

4. Watch your thoughts for a few minutes and try to categorise them into past present and future. Now roughly calculate what percentage of time you spend in each time zone. Are you a mainly past focused, present focussed or future focussed person? What causes

you the most stress – thinking about what has happened, what is happening or what might happen?

5. What could you use as a rose in your life? Choose some triggers that will instantly remind you of the need to spend more time enjoying the present, rather than stewing over what has happened or worrying about what might happen.

AWARENESS

IN THIRTY WORDS OR LESS...

'Self observation develops awareness
which provides us with
information from which we can
fashion creative expectations and
Enlightened Responses.'

---

*'If I have no expectations
about what might happen and no
opinions and judgements
about what is happening or has
happened, then I am free to
peacefully observe any situation.'*

CHAPTER SEVEN

SELF OBSERVATION – IN REAL LIFE

By Self Observation, I not only mean objectively watching my thoughts and behaviours, but also the myriad other events and follow-on effects which emanate from me as the centre of my world. If I am one with the world, made of the same stuff and for the same ultimate and as yet unknown grand purpose, then the world is also one with me. Like the pebble thrown into the pond that causes ripples to seek out the farthest corners of that pond, I cannot interact with my world without in some way altering its course. And the reverse is also true. My expectations are certainly an integral part of the process of creating events in my pond. But just as certainly, events occurring further out in the pond, or indeed in other people's ponds, send waves back toward me – waves that I need to evaluate and respond to. A smoother, more enjoyable life requires that I be vigilant and observe the various ripples and waves that roll to and from the shores of my pond.

Where do I start?

To begin with, it is probably useful for you to know that, as with life, there really are no right or wrong ways to practise self observation. But – and isn't there always a 'but'? – there are a couple of basic principles that, if you choose to adhere to them, will make your practice more effective.

Principle One: Focus

Whatever you choose for your focus, whenever your mind wanders from it, gently but firmly coax it back.

My mind is like a small child; it loves distractions, dreams, wishes, places to go and things to do. As a caring adult I need to teach my child when and how to focus so that he may become a productive and fulfilled member of the community. My mind needs the same supportive guidelines.

The sort of dialogue that occurs in my mind when my thoughts stray, goes something like this:

Focussed mind: 'OK, Following my breathing. Not labelling it or judging it; merely observing it.'

Wandering Mind: 'Hey! That sounds like a Volkswagen, just like ours. I wonder if it is ours. We need petrol if we're going away tomorrow. Did I ring Diana to let her know what time we're leaving? When I've finished here I'll...'

Focussed mind: 'Thank you for alerting me to those things, but that's not what we're doing right now. Back to observing my breathing.'

Wandering Mind: 'But what if she doesn't know...

Focussed mind: 'Thank you, but we're staying here with my breathing and we'll deal with that later... my breathing... my breathing... my breath... my breath... my breath...'

...and on ad infinitum.

Principle Two: Practise, practise, practise, practise...
Where can I practise?

Where you practise is far less important than how often. Buses, bus stops, trains and railway stations, doctors' waiting rooms, churches – any denomination, any time as they are usually nice and quiet – parks and gardens, beaches... the list is as endless as your imagination. If you can look at everything that goes on around you as just part of your environment rather than a distraction away from it, then you are truly on your way to learning acceptance of *what is* rather than going into judgement because of how you think things *should be*. Events such as people rushing about, mobile phones, traffic noise and next door's lawn mower, are around all the time; and if you are to develop an air of calm productivity, whatever your surroundings, you will eventually need to get used to them. But particularly when starting out, it is often easier to choose somewhere that is quiet and free from distractions.

I mentioned earlier that I spent some time with the monks at the

Bhutia Busty Monastery in Darjeeling, India. The answer to my innocent question about the Lama's meditation techniques has been ringing in my ears since that moment, so I guess it is important enough to repeat here.

'My friend', he said, 'my whole life is a meditation'. At that instant my head was filled with the prospect of each and every minute of my life being a source of enlightenment, if only I could learn to see the lessons.

We talked at length on many subjects (including the then current cricket series between India and Australia) but the essence of the teaching for me was summed up in just one of his sentences.

> *'Anything I do with one hundred percent*
> *mindfulness is a meditation.'*

Be aware of your breathing

I will be liberally scattering the acronym BAOYB&J – be aware of your breathing and jaw – throughout the following observation scripts. The pace and depth of your breathing and the tightness of your jaw are both reasonably accurate indicators of your current state of tension, or relaxation, whatever the case may be. Check them now before you continue reading. Is your breathing slow, deep and even, or shallow and erratic? Is your jaw tense or relaxed?

Have you ever noticed how we tend to *catch our breath* – an almost involuntary or sudden stop – when we are surprised or frightened by something? It is all a part of our *Fight or Flight* reaction to danger and is designed to protect us. But with the constant attack of trivia that our minds strangely perceive as life threatening, we are on perpetual alert. Many muscles actually tighten in these moments, or strings of moments, and your jaw can serve as an indicator of what's happening elsewhere in your body. Once you are aware of this mind-body process, you can begin to short-circuit it by diverting your energy into more productive or creative areas. Gently relax your jaw and face muscles and allow your breathing to settle back into a slow, deep and even rhythm. It will only take a few seconds, but your body will thank you forever. So remember – BAOYB&J

69

Where are your thoughts?

Self-explanatory really. But to highlight the importance of this point...

You will need to be vigilant that your thoughts stay focussed on whatever you have chosen. Your mind is used to having it's own way and initially will not take kindly to being harnessed. In every situation, in every waking moment I find it useful to ask myself: 'Where are my thoughts?' And if they have wandered, I gently coax them back to where I want them.

Choosing a Focus for <u>YOUR</u> Observations

And I emphasise the word <u>your</u> focus because it will most likely be different from <u>my</u> focus.

Note: If you read nothing else in this book except this first observation, you will have all the basic information you need to create the life you want, using the awarenesses you gather as a firm foundation.

Environmental Observation

Your environment is wherever you happen to be. With all the talk about 'the environment' recently, it would be easy to conclude that by the term Environmental Observation, I am referring to an activity performed in a natural setting, or smoke free environment or at least a healthy environment. Not so! This self observation can be practised ANYWHERE!

> *'If I can take the attitude that I am simply an observer of my life, then no matter what happens around me, it is all part of my environment at that moment.'*

This has been a most valuable tool for me for avoiding being drawn into judgement of events, people or situations. As an observer of my life, my task is simply to be aware of what is going on in the moment, without expectations. And so...

> *'If I have no expectations about what might happen and no opinions and judgements about what is happening or has happened, then I am free to peacefully observe any situation.'*

And in <u>YOUR</u> life...

1. Take a moment to really focus on your present environment and begin to fully appreciate the only moment you have any control over; and even that is limited.

2. Now spend at least a few minutes screening out the rest of your environment and focus only on your process of breathing. There are very few people who can do this exercise and still not feel at least partially relaxed.

SELF OBSERVATION IN REAL LIFE

IN THIRTY WORDS OR LESS...

'Non-judgemental observation of simple everyday events will help to fine-tune our awareness – the more we choose to see, the more we will learn to see, until reality becomes visible.'

*'The honest objectivity of
being able to impartially observe
the state of your own emotions,
and not judge them, will be
a major step toward creating
more peace in your life.'*

CHAPTER EIGHT

OBSERVATION SCRIPTS

Variations on a theme

All the scenarios in this chapter are merely extensions and variations of the Basic Environmental Observation. They have been written as suggestions of how to practically go about the process of observing your life. I suggest that you read through the fifty scripts relatively quickly to give you an overview of the sort of things to look for in your daily routine. Then, while still reading the rest of the book, take a new script each day, focus on the fine details, and add your own personal observations as you go. You will probably be amazed at just how quickly you amass information and understanding of how and why you do the things you do. Enjoy the journey!

It will also help to keep the two principles in mind:

Focus and Practise. (…and, oh yeah, don't forget to enjoy!)

1. The Basic Environmental Observation

Begin by making yourself as comfortable as possible. You may be sitting in a quiet park, in a busy cafe, in your own bed, your office, or even standing on a crowded train. Wherever you are is perfect.

Take a deep breath in and as you let it out, gently close your eyes. Don't force them shut as this places tension on the muscles and skin around the eyes.

Important Note: An estimated 80% of the information reaching our brain comes through our eyes. It would seem logical to screen out that information while we are learning to master any mind management techniques. Learning to focus is like restricting yourself to only reading one letter at a time instead or opening and sorting all your mail simultaneously. In some circumstances it may not be practical or appropriate to close your eyes. In this case, just follow all the instructions as best you can with your eyes open.

Hear

Now let your mind have it's way for a moment, examining and getting used to it's new sightless environment. Be aware of how many different sounds you can hear. Notice that the longer you focus on sounds the more you will hear and the more sensitive your ears will become. Be especially aware of judgement creeping in.

> *'Nothing is intrinsically good or bad
> except that we choose to make it so.'*
> OLD TAOIST PROVERB

It's a bit like the binary system of modern computers in which every single piece of information is given a value of either 0 or 1, and processed accordingly. In our thinking, things are mostly labelled 'Good' or 'Bad' or perhaps 'Right' or 'Wrong,' but very rarely 'Neutral'.

Try not to even label the sounds you hear, for in doing so you may inadvertently slip into judgement. For example, if you hear a robin sing, and you happen to like robins, then you will have a positive reaction when you label it, 'Robin'. On the other hand, if you hate crows and happen to hear one and label it, you will immediately have an irritating thought that is accompanied by a physical response. Every thought you have produces a physical reaction in your body – and isn't that a scary thought?!

Feel

Next, turn your awareness to your sense of touch, and I don't just mean your fingers.

What can you feel on or in your body? The warmth of the sun, coolness of shade, clothes against your skin, rumbling stomach, full bladder, socks and shoes against your feet. Run your tongue around your teeth and feel their smoothness along with the wetness or dryness of your mouth. Feel the sensation of breath entering your nostrils, against the back of your throat and travelling deep into your lungs. Feel your diaphragm move and your body expand to accommodate the air you have sucked in. For a couple of breaths, when you exhale, feel the air rising from your diaphragm, through your chest, your throat and blow out through a slightly opened mouth feeling the air rushing over your lips. Scan the muscles and organs of your body and be aware of any feelings of either comfort or discomfort or even the muscles working to hold your present position. You could spend hours just mentally exploring your body, if that's where you decide to direct your focus.

Smell

What can you smell in the air? Notice each different type of smell without labelling it, and then move on to the next one. Be careful that your mind doesn't pick up a thought and run with it. For example, a chain of thoughts triggered by the smell of bacon might lead to: 'Yum, I like bacon...mmm... my mouth's watering... I'm really hungry... I wonder what the time is... maybe it's dinner time!... I wonder who's cooking it… if there's some left I'd like to...'

Taste

What can you taste in your mouth? Again, be mindful of any need to follow a thought. Like, 'Oh no! My mouth tastes terrible. I wish I'd cleaned my teeth before I started.'

Think

Where are your thoughts? Are you finding it easy to stay with the self observation or is your mind trying to hijack the whole process and take you off to something more exciting or perhaps to something you're worried about? Remember to just observe what's happening and not get hooked into self-flagellation for not being able to stay focussed. Gently coax it back to where you want it.

Feel Emotionally

And where are your emotions? How do you feel right now? It is quite likely that, in the course of your day, many people will ask you what you *think* about something, but very few people will ask you what you *feel*. Are you happy, sad, excited, bored, manic, depressed or completely neutral?

'The honest objectivity of being able to impartially observe the state of your own emotions, and not judge them, will be a major step toward creating more peace in your life.'

See

Slowly start opening your eyes and become aware of everything in the almost 180 degrees of your vision, not focussing on any one thing but generally taking in everything around you. I call it a 'soft focus'. Be aware of light and shade... be aware of colour... notice how there are different shades of the same colour... be aware of texture and your ability to combine sight with memory to know how something would feel if you touched it... be aware of size... and shape... and distance... and notice any movement... or the stillness... and now focus your mind on your breath and follow it deep into your body... and finally, scan your body, noticing your muscles and any areas of tension, consciously relaxing those areas and gradually bring yourself back to an awareness of where you are and what you need to do next.

If you have sufficient time, close your eyes and return to the beginning... What can you hear...

The physical awarenesses gained by monitoring our senses are useful in themselves, but as a method for teaching us to become more aware of our thoughts and emotions, they are invaluable.

It is definitely worth repeating something I mentioned earlier:

'If I have control over my thoughts and emotions, I effectively have control over my entire life.'

The brief version

Get comfortable		Close your eyes
Ask yourself:	What can I	HEAR?
	What can I	FEEL? (Physically)
	What can I	FEEL? (Emotionally)
	What can I	TASTE?
	What can I	SMELL?
	What am I	THINKING?
Open your eyes	What can I	SEE? (soft focus – 180 degrees)

...in any order, in any combination and for any length of time that works for you. And remember that:

'The importance is placed on the TASK of focus, not the SUBJECT of focus.'

Real Life Scripts
2. Breath Awareness

This is by far the most widely used form of self observation in the world. Called Pranyama by the Indian Yoga teachers, its most simple form can be described as a method of focussing on the breath. I will detail a couple of mind scripts for you to try, but you will probably develop a style that works for you.

To extol the virtues of breathing would seem initially to be unnecessary, after all, we all know that if we stop, we will die. But deep rhythmical breathing has long been underestimated as a tool for physical and mental relaxation. When you think about it, over 80% of our body is estimated to be composed of water, and one glance at the chemical formula H_2O will tell you that a fair proportion of that is Oxygen. Oxygen is one of the major building blocks of our body and the chief method for extracting it from the air around us is...? You guessed it; breathing! Add to that the fact that our minds and bodies love rhythm, probably because one of the first sensations we experience in the womb is the rhythmical beating of our mother's heart. Scientists believe it is also the reason we like music, dancing, chanting ... and so many other of those rhythm based 'ing' words. The slow, constant, repetitive flow of air to and from our lungs can be a marvellous natural tool for calming the whole collection of physical, mental and emotional processes which constitute our lives. (BAOYB&J)

To begin with, choose a location where you feel relaxed and hopefully won't be disturbed for a while – a quiet room, a corner of the garden or even on a forest trail. Sit with your back straight, either in a chair or crossed legged on the floor or ground. Another variation is to sit with your buttocks on a cushion or a low stool and your legs crossed in front of you. Rehearsing the process over and over will enable you to practice this form of self observation just about anywhere, but to start with, the more comfortable you are and fewer distractions you have, the easier it will be to maintain your focus.

Take a deep breath in and as you let it out, gently close your eyes. Don't force them shut as this places tension on the muscles and skin around the eyes. Let your mind have its way for a moment, examining and getting used to its new environment.

What can you hear, feel, smell and taste? Gradually become aware of your breath. Mentally follow it into your body through your nose. Your nose not only filters the air as it enters your body, but also warms it so that it is the right temperature for your lungs. (BAOYB&J)

Become aware of the whole breathing process. Feel the air pass through your nostrils and hit the back of your throat as it is sucked down into your lungs by your diaphragm. Notice how your chest rises and falls with each breath and your ribs expand and separate. Your diaphragm (the wall of muscle just below your ribcage) will also move with each breath as it expands like a blacksmith's bellows to accommodate the increased volume of air. Be mindful of the rhythm of the breath, noticing if it speeds up or slows down or becomes deeper. Constantly return to the breath each time you are distracted away from your focus.

*Diligent self observation leads to awareness
which forms the basis for building
creative expectations and the choosing of
enlightened responses.*

3. Breathing Colours

Imagine the air you are breathing has a colour. You may want to choose your favourite colour or one that gives you a feeling of peace or relaxation. It may be the colour of the sky or a favourite room or even an article of clothing. Imagine the breath entering through your nose and see this colour flow deep into your body, colouring your lungs and your diaphragm. (Your diaphragm is that section of muscle just below your rib cage that acts as a bellows arrangement to suck air into your body and your lungs.) Now see the air flow from your body with the out-breath. You may even want to change the colour of the out-breath. This can sometimes signify that the out breath is carrying away things that you don't need; like stress, pain, muscle tightness or negative and non-productive thoughts. (BAOYB&J)

With each successive breath you might feel yourself becoming more and more relaxed or visualise the colour of an area of discomfort becoming smaller and less intense.

4. Counting Breaths

Sometimes our minds are so active that focussing seems almost impossible for more than a few seconds. And some of us experience this all the time! For these situations it is sometimes useful to count the breaths – giving the mind another task makes it less likely to want to wander. (BAOYB&J)

Most people find it easier to start with a cycle of say, five breaths. At the completion of the five, you simply return to *one* and start again. You may want to progress to ten breaths or any number that seems to suit you. With practice I have noticed that my breathing pattern quickly settles into a cycle of ten breaths per minute. This enables me to predetermine the length of my self observation session. If I only have ten minutes I simply set my mental breath counter at One Hundred breaths and I don't have to worry about setting an alarm or whether or not I'm going to miss an appointment. Calculating your own breathing rate will assist you to monitor your progress. (BAOYB&J)

5. Breath Visualisations

Combine your breathing with mental imagery. (BAOYB&J)

i) One of my favourites is to picture myself sitting on a beach watching the waves roll in toward me. Sometimes I synchronise the waves with my breathing, and if I am counting, I usually superimpose the number of each breath on to the wave.

ii) With each breath, focus on a different colour of the rainbow. The seven colours – red, orange, yellow, green, blue, indigo, violet – can also match up with a seven-breath cycle. My experience with this is that with each set of seven, the breaths often become deeper and longer and the colours more vivid.

iii) Did you know that the old 'counting sheep' is actually a visualisation? (or meditation) Any variation on this is possible from counting apples to aardvarks. See how creative you can be! (BAOYB&J)

6. Walking

Another of my personal favourites is to practise while walking along a deserted beach. But no matter where or when you are walking, the same basic principles apply. Focus on observation, not judgement or opinion.

Be aware of the sights, smells and sounds of the environment in which you have chosen to walk. I often use the mental script of: 'What can I see.... hear.... feel.... smell.... taste ', in a type of rolling self observation, almost like a Mantra (see explanation of Mantras and Chanting – before No 28) In a natural setting, such as a forest or beach, it can greatly enhance your awareness of the environment by allowing you to notice many things that you might ordinarily miss. (BAOYB&J)

You will be creating your own audible presence too. Listen to the sound of your breathing, and sometimes you will also notice the noise of blood rushing through your head, depending on how hard you're working. Listen to the sound of your feet contacting the ground and even your clothes will make slight rustling sounds as your legs brush together and arms swish against the sides of your body.

Be aware of the muscles you use to propel you along. Notice the swing of your hips as you project your legs forward. What do your arms do as you walk? Experiment with your length of step and how high your arms swing. Be aware of your breath and how it coordinates with your step.

Another variation can be used indoors or in an enclosed area, similar to the way the Buddhists walk in clockwise circles around a Stupa (religious monument). The self observation is exactly as above but you can add the counting of steps to keep your mind focussed and you don't have to worry about traffic or keeping track of your direction. (BAOYB&J)

Walking on uneven ground or a bush track has the added advantage of being great exercise for your eyes, having to change focus rapidly to work out where your next step should be. It is also good for your sense of balance as having to shift weight and change direction so often, brings different muscle groups into play that would not normally be used on flat or even ground. From a meditative viewpoint it gives you more to keep your mind occupied, which is a bonus for those of us who struggle to remain focussed.

7. Running

Start with the basic Environmental Observation.

You will be creating your own audible presence too. Listen to the sound of your breathing and sometimes you will also notice the sound of blood rushing through your head, depending on how hard you're working. Listen to the sound of your feet contacting the ground and even your clothes will make slight rustling sounds as your legs brush together and arms swish against the sides of your body.

Be aware of the muscles in use to propel you along. Notice the swing of your hips as you project your legs forward. What do your arms do as you run? Experiment with your length of step and how high your arms swing. Be aware of your breath and how it coordinates with your running rhythm. (BAOYB&J)

You can add the counting of steps or breaths to keep your mind focussed.

Running on uneven ground or a bush track has the added advantage of being great exercise for your eyes having to change focus rapidly to work out where your next step should be. It is also good for your sense of balance and having to shift weight and change direction so often brings different muscle groups into play that would not normally be used on flat or even ground. From a meditative viewpoint it gives you more to keep your mind occupied, which is a bonus for those of us who struggle to remain focussed. (BAOYB&J)

8. Sitting

Be aware of the sights, smells and sounds of the environment in which you have chosen to sit. I often use the mental script of: 'What can I see.... hear.... feel.... smell.... taste', in a type of rolling self observation, almost like a Mantra (see explanation of Mantras and Chanting – before No 28) In a natural setting, such as a forest or beach, it can greatly enhance your awareness of the environment by allowing you to notice many things which you might ordinarily miss.

In an office or work environment it can help reduce your need to make judgements by working on acceptance of your surroundings as not good or bad, boring or exciting, man-made instead of natural: it is just the way it is. (BAOYB&J)

Once you have satisfied your wandering mind with a scan of your environment, turn your focus on to your body, starting at your toes and working up through your feet, legs, buttocks and groin, hips, stomach, back, chest, arms, neck, throat, chin, back of neck, jaw, face, back of your head, eyes and top of your head.

9. Standing (and/or waiting)

How many times have you been left on a corner, at a bus stop, in a foyer or at a train station, waiting for someone or something? I've lost count. But this can be a great opportunity to become aware of your immediate environment, and in particular, how your body reacts to just 'standing around'.

Start with an Environmental Observation and then...

(BAOYB&J) Feel the weight of your body forcing down into your shoes and into the ground beneath you. What you are feeling is actually the effects of gravity pulling you towards the centre of the earth. Contemplate that for a moment. Gravity is the tendency of two bodies to be attracted towards each other. This is an interaction between you and planet earth! Feel which muscles are tightening and loosening to keep you upright. Your tendency to fall if you lean too far is merely gravity pulling the top half of your body past the bottom half of your body. (BAOYB&J) The muscles and bones of your body work in harmony to keep your torso balanced over your hips legs and feet. It is a constant and relentless battle going on all day and every day while we are standing or sitting. The only rest we have from this struggle is when we lay down. Is it any wonder that we need to get horizontal and sleep at the end of a long day on our feet? Focus your observation on every tiny muscular twitch, every area of pain, discomfort, stress or pleasure. Feel your neck muscles holding your head up. Notice the muscles in your feet and how much control they have over your balance. (BAOYB&J) Are your arms hanging limply at your side or are they tense, moving rigidly with your torso as you turn or bend?

Still more time to wait? Then go back to the Environmental Observation – there's plenty going on that you probably missed the first time!

10. Eating

Eating is much more than just a taste sensation, twenty-eight chews, a swallow and a contented feeling when you've finished. It often starts with the aroma wafting from the kitchen. Be aware of the effect these smells have on your taste buds. Are your salivary glands reacting? Can you identify the different odours? What visual stimulation does the food offer? Colours, patterns, textures? How is it presented or arranged? What about the serving dish or plate? Be aware of its colour and texture as well – whether it's fine bone china or a brown paper bag. (BAOYB&J) How does the food feel? Is it something you handle with your fingers or pick up with cutlery? And even if you don't touch it with your bare hands, imagine how it would feel if you did touch it. Does it cut or separate easily? Does it stay on your fork or spoon or does it want to fall off? Notice the sensations as the first mouthful reaches your lips and then your tongue. Be aware of the way your tongue pushes the food from side to side in your mouth to enable the cutting and crushing of your teeth. How many times do you need to chew before habit or practicality dictates that it is time to swallow? Can you mentally trace the mouthful down into your body, feeling its progress? Be aware of your body telling you that you've probably had enough. (BAOYB&J) Enjoy that blissful period between when the hunger stops and the indigestion starts! Do you perhaps eat too fast or too much or without appreciation because your thoughts are elsewhere?

11. Body-watching (Your own, not someone else's!)

I suggest starting with your hands. Do you fully appreciate how marvellous they are? Billions of dollars of research, design, engineering and technology have been as yet unable to create something even close to attaining their levels of dexterity and endurance. From the fine adjustments required by a watchmaker to the strength for carrying heavy suitcases, your hands work almost tirelessly for at least sixteen hours each day. But how often do you consciously appreciate their magnificence? (BAOYB&J)

Make a fist in front of your face and slowly begin to unfold each finger,

one at a time. Notice how slowly you can do this. Now one at a time, wriggle each finger independently of the others and notice the full extent of their arc of movement. Change your focus to your wrists and rotate each hand, firstly toward you and then away from you, being aware of where this movement starts. The muscles that enable this range of movement are actually in your forearm and originate near your elbow. Can you trace them back that far, or even further? If you hold your right bicep with your left hand while rotating your right hand, can you accomplish that without feeling any tension in that right bicep? Move both hands up and down in a waving motion without moving your forearm and again ascertain how much travel is possible from the 'fully down' position to the 'fully up'. Experiment with making different shapes with your fingers and notice how little or how much pressure can be applied by squeezing one hand with the other. Like your breath, your hands are ever present and can serve as an ideal focus to instantly bring your thoughts into the present moment. (BAOYB&J)

If time permits, repeat this observation with other parts of your body, being aware of type and range of movement and which muscles are involved. Or for a quick session, just select one area or limb to focus on.

12. Cleaning your teeth

Feel the weight of the brush in your hand. With which hand do you hold it and what is your other hand doing at the same time? Which fingers actually grip the brush? Is it smooth or does it have one of those rubbery grips? Feel the toothpaste tube or bottle in your opposite hand as you pick it up. The weight, texture, size. What do your fingers do to get the toothpaste out of its container? How much do you put on the brush and where? In the middle? At one end? A thin strip down the centre of the bristles? Or does it cover the whole brush head? (BAOYB&J) As you lift the brush into your mouth do you look into the mirror or just stare out into space? Which teeth do you start brushing first?... and where next?... and after that? Feel the bristles against your teeth and gums. Taste the toothpaste. Are you an 'up and down' brusher or a 'round and round' brusher? How long do you brush for? Is there a set routine that you need to complete before you feel satisfied that the task is finished? Do you just go over this routine once?... twice? ...or is there just some areas you need to go over a second or third time? Feel the temperature of the water in your mouth as you rinse out the toothpaste. How long do you take to rinse the brush and how do you remove the excess water from it? Are you a flicker, a wiper or a tapper? (BAOYB&J)

13. Cycling

I received my first bicycle for Christmas, just before my twelfth birthday and have owned one almost continuously since. There is something about rolling those first few feet down the driveway that instantly carries me back to my teens and the excitement and freedom of having my own transport. It was my licence to explore my ever-widening world.

First and foremost: Be aware of the traffic, road rules and road conditions and always, always keep your own safety and the safety of others uppermost in your mind. (BAOYB&J)

Feel the coolness of the metal handlebars and the texture of the tyres as you check the tyre pressures. Feel the weight of your feet on the pedals, saddle against your sitting bones and hands on the handlebars. Notice how you move your weight from side to side to maintain balance as you ride. (BAOYB&J) Notice how your body's cooling system chimes in and produces perspiration to cool you down. Try to create a breathing pattern which coordinates your breaths with the rotation of the pedals and notice how this changes as riding becomes more difficult. – up hills or into the wind. The rhythm of riding a bike is ideal for experimenting with mantras and repetitive phrases, which help to focus the mind. I find them particularly useful on long slow hills. While mentally reciting a mantra (See section on Mantras before No. 28) I visually skim over the road surface, sometimes imagining I'm flying, or picturing each grain or pebble of rock in the road surface as a person. It helps me to appreciate that I am a small part of something that is so enormous and complex. It helps to foster humility.

14. Driving

As my work takes me to various parts of the world and quite often into large cities, I often find myself behind the steering wheel of a car. City driving being similar – i.e. potentially stressful – in most countries, I find I have numerous opportunities to practise Self Observation. While being ever mindful of the traffic, dangers, road rules etc, I still find it useful to start with an Environmental Observation. And then...

(BAOYB&J) Feel your hands on the steering wheel. Are you gripping it tightly or loosely and relaxed? Explore the texture of the wheel and if appropriate (e.g. If stuck in traffic or waiting for a traffic light to change) run your fingers lightly along the surface being aware of indentations or slight imperfections. Does it have a hard surface or is it soft and spongey? As your hand operates the gear lever, be aware of any resistance. Does it move easily form one gear to another or is there an element of 'clunkiness'? Watch how the light falls on the interior of the vehicle, reflecting off some areas and forming shadows on others. Listen to the sounds of the motor and gearbox (without judgement – not looking for noises which may lead to expensive repair bills!) and also to the sounds all around the car. Other cars, trucks, birds, children playing, people talking, machinery operating... all without judgement. None of them good or bad, but just the way they are. (BAOYB&J)

15. Gardening

This is a great place to start with an Environmental Observation. Notice how the light plays on the ground, the rocks, grass, plants... Feel the texture of your gloves (if you wear them) and the weight and texture of the tools you are using. As you disturb the earth, be aware of the moisture content and again, the texture of the soil. Are there any insects, worms, or other animals present? Be careful of any judgements that creep in, about the quality of the soil, what you shouldn't or should have done, whether the insects are good or bad or even be aware of favouring one type of plant over another. (BAOYB&J)

If you are watering, watch how the droplets catch the light. Follow one from the end of the hose or watering can to where it lands. What happens when it hits the surface of a plant or some other object? Watch to see if it soaks in or sits on the surface, or if it begins to form rivulets and then small pools or puddles. And what happens when the light strikes these tiny areas of water? While pruning trees, feel the weight and temperature of the cutters in your hand. Notice how your hand opens and closes to operate the implement and the way your eyes and hand co-ordinate to take the cutters to your chosen point on the stem and feel the tension as the blades slice through it. Does any sap escape from the cut surfaces and if so, what colour is it? (BAOYB&J)

If you are mowing, be aware of all the smells, sounds, vibrations and sights that accompany this task. Observe the patterns created by the mowers cutting blades on the lawn and note the trajectory of the pieces of severed grass as they are flung away from the machine. Smell the cut grass. Focus on the droning rhythm of the motor and notice how the pitch of the note it plays alters with the amount of exertion it needs to make.

16. Bathing

(BAOYB&J)Be aware of the change in temperature as you remove your clothes. Feel the tension of the taps as you turn them on and adjust the temperature of the water. If you use bath salts or some form of bubble-bath mixture, watch how it affects the water, how the bubbles form and the way they spread across the surface. Be aware of the sounds of the bath filling, the warmth rising from it, the smells present and the movement of water, steam, bubbles or even any float-ing toys (yours or your children's!) As your toes first enter, absorb fully the sensations of warmth and wetness and also be aware of which muscles are in action to lower you into the water. Notice how much of what you do now is out of habit. Do you lay back and fully immerse yourself, luxuriating in the pleasant sensation of the warm envelopment and semi-weightlessness? Or do you throw yourself headlong into the task with your mind off somewhere in the past or future? How do you wash yourself? What do you use and what part of your body do you start on? Are some parts more sensitive and more pleasurable to wash than others? Watch your thoughts and emotions as you follow this simple and quite natural observation and acknowledgement. The human body was designed to respond to touch, with some areas far more responsive than others. So why is it that some of us feel guilty when we receive pleasure from our own touch. If it wasn't meant to feel good, then surely it wouldn't. Nothing else in our bodies or in our range of senses seems to have occurred by chance, so it only seems natural to assume that tactile pleasure is just as it was planned. (BAOYB&J)

What can you hear? Does the water slosh around you as you wash yourself? Can you hear the tinkling as tiny drops fall back into the bath? Listen to the different pitch of the musical notes created, depending on the size of the water droplets hitting the surface. (BAOYB&J) As you breathe in, be aware of the smell of soap or what-ever else lingers in the air. When you have finished bathing, remove the plug from the drain and become aware of your body losing its weight-lessness as the water level recedes. Enjoy the sensation of towelling off.

17. Showering

Be aware of the change in temperature as you remove your clothes. Feel the tension of the taps as you turn the shower on and adjust the temperature of the water. Feel the rush of air as the water displaces it from the shower cubicle. Notice how the light catches the water droplets and mentally note what happens as theses droplets hit the walls or floor of the shower. As you step under the flow of water be mindful of the different sensations that occur. (BAOYB&J) Feel the temperature of the water and sensation of each tiny jet striking your skin. Enjoy the trickling feeling as the water cascades over your body toward the floor. Whether you use a wash-cloth or just soap, be aware of the texture against your skin. Notice how some areas are more sen-sitive than others and how the closer you get to the shower head, the warmer the water is. By the time the drops reach your feet, they have cooled markedly. As you turn the taps off you will notice the change in temperature as the air contacts your wet skin. Feel the texture of the towel as it soaks up the excess water and notice the clean, refreshed sensation and the tingling of the skin if you rub it briskly with the towel. (BAOYB&J)

18. Swimming

(BAOYB&J) What you experience while swimming has much to do with where you are swimming. A chlorinated pool will give a far dif-ferent set of observations than a dip in the surf. But as always with self observations, the principles are the same. As you near the water, start with an Environmental Observation and then narrow your focus to your immediate environment just before entering. Be aware of every muscle involved in propelling you through the water and the temper-ature against your skin. What can you taste and smell and how does the water feel against your skin? Notice the light patterns both above and below the water and the way the reflections in the water are con-stantly disturbed by your movements. As gravity is attempting to pull you down, your body's own buoyancy is working to push you up to the surface. Experiment with this feeling of comparative weightless-ness allowing the water to support you. Now compare this to your life. Do you allow your friends and family to support you, or are you a strong and independent 'I don't need anyone' person? Do you allow *life* itself to support you? i.e. Do you go with the flow or struggle against the current? Remember to stay focussed on *you* in this deviation from your present physical environment, not allowing your thoughts to spin off into other people's lives but staying with your own interactions with the world around you.

(BAOYB&J) By necessity, your breathing while you swim will change. Watch how your body compensates for this new set of circumstances, holding the air in your lungs while submerged and then taking in deep breaths when you can. Do you lift your head completely out of the water as you swim or just turn your open mouth until it is above the surface? How long can you hold it or how many strokes can you make with one breath? If you exhale under the water, how does that feel and can you notice the bubbles move across your lips and against your face and body? Are your eyes open under the water and how clearly can you make out the objects around you? If you keep your eyes closed, what does your imagination see? Do you picture your surroundings and where you are or just blackness? Finally, as you leave the water, be aware of the sensation of your weight increasing, the water dripping from you, the temperature of the air, the ground under your feet, your breathing rate and the soft brushing of the towel as it soaks the excess water from your skin.

19. Listening to Music

Traditionally, music for self observation, relaxation or meditation has been soft, slow and repetitive, lulling the senses into a quiet, hypnotic state. And if the slowing of thought processes and heart rates is what's required, then this style of music is ideal. But for the purposes of mind focus and learning to stay in the present moment, any music will suffice. (BAOYB&J)

Start by differentiating between the instruments used, but be careful not to label them. Your past experiences will colour any attitudes you have toward these instruments – some you may like and others not. Just see them as different sounds and appreciate there varying tones, pitches, rhythms and whether they dominate the overall sound picture or subtly blend into the background. Be aware of melodious sounds, percussive sounds, loud, soft, slow, fast. Experiment with attributing colours to the vast array of musical notes you hear, and notice if they have any particular effect on your moods. How do these differing sounds make you feel? Let the music wash over you. (BAOYB&J) After you have scanned the whole musical spectrum, isolating certain sounds and beats, try to hear the entire production as one solid but flowing entity, almost as if it is one giant, multi-faceted but fluid musical note. Attempt to ride with it as it climbs and falls. Play with your imagination, creating pictures that flow with the music, swirling, turning and changing as it bounces along. Be aware of the effects that different types of music have on these mind pictures so that in the future you can choose the type of imaginary journey you want.

20. Washing dishes

This is another of those daily, repetitive and often solo chores that lends itself readily to self observation. Feel the weight, texture and temperature of the cutlery as you separate it from the crockery and cooking utensils. Be careful not to judge the smells of leftovers and the dirty plates (which is easy to do when your stomach is full). Notice the smell of the washing up liquid and steam rising from the hot water as it tumbles into the sink. Feel the warmth as your hands carry the first item into the water and also the texture of the dishcloth or brush. (BAOYB&J) What sounds can you hear? Water sloshing, plates and cutlery scraping the sides of the washing bowl or sink, the almost inaudible hiss of detergent bubbles bursting. How do you feel about the water becoming murky and getting worse as more dishes are washed? And what thoughts did you have to trigger these feelings. I think we sometimes tackle this job with an expectation that the water will stay clear and clean until the last dish, otherwise why would we get irritated or disappointed that we have to refill the sink, or why do we turn up our noses in disgust at the filthy state of the water? (BAOYB&J)

If you place the dishes in a rack to drain, watch the effect that gravity has, drawing the droplets down towards the draining board and eventually forming small streams bound for the drain hole. (If it doesn't, speak to your plumber quick!) If you dry your dishes manually, be aware of the weight of each item as you pick it up and the way the light catches it as you move it through the air. Does the tea towel or drying cloth have an odour? (awareness, not judgement) Feel the dryness of the towel and notice how it slowly becomes moist as you use it, soaking up the water from the dishes. Be aware of your own dexterity as you skilfully locate, pick up, handle, dry and store each item. (BAOYB&J)

You can of course do a shorter version of this observation while loading and unloading a dishwasher and tidying the kitchen.

21. Preparing Food

Few observations are better than this one for combining all the faculties into an eclectic symphony of sensory stimulation. It starts for me as I shop for the ingredients of the meal I intend to prepare. The sight of fresh fruit and vegetables stacked in colourful displays at the supermarket or greengrocer is always visually exciting to me. Couple this with the aroma of the herb and spice aisle and my taste buds are already in motion preparing for the prospective feast.

Once you have everything you need lined up in your kitchen, (your observation having restarted as you collected the items from the refrigerator and cupboards) your focus then depends very much on the menu you have chosen. Washing and then chopping, grating or peeling vegetables can be an absorbing process. It is certainly a tactile experience and should also stimulate your nose with the aromas, causing your salivary glands to step up production in anticipation. (BAOYB&J)

Some individual items, like garlic, onions or lemons, will have a greater effect than others. Be also aware of the physical properties of the foods as you prepare them. Are they brittle or flexible? Do they bend or snap? Are they juicy inside or dry? And what happens when you start to cook them? Do the aromas get stronger or the physical qualities change? Do the firm ones become soft, limp ones go crisp or do the solid ones liquefy? Notice how the colours alter as the cooking process advances – some becoming pale and others intensifying. Do all the ingredients eventually blend together so that the finished item is a single entity or do some stay intact – part of the whole but still keeping their individuality? Or perhaps some of them partially disappear leaving only seeds or pieces of skin to indicate their presence? When serving the meal, do you arrange the individual portions into their own neat segments on the plate? Is the blend of colours visually stimulating? (BAOYB&J)

22. Sitting in a restaurant or café

There is so much happening in a restaurant or café – it really is an 'observers paradise'. People-watching is a favourite pastime for most of us, but how often do we focus on our own reactions to, and involvement with, the surroundings, and our interactions with this bustling social environment? (BAOYB&J)

Begin to notice the continual drone of voices and chatter. Become aware of the sounds that rise above this background murmur – cutlery tinkling, glasses clinking, bottles in ice buckets, kitchen doors swinging, music playing. Observe how your sense of sight is bombarded with a kaleidoscope of colours, shapes, textures, light and shade. Run your soft gaze over the carpets, drapes, wall colours, clothes, tablecloths, napkins, menus, food and furniture. (BAOYB&J) Notice the constant sea of movement – people walking, sitting, leaning, eating, nodding, gesticulating, chewing. Observe your own table – the arrangement of the cutlery, table decorations, glasses. What are the different smells you can identify and what effect do they have on your taste buds? Which smells attract you and which repel? Be aware of yourself eating (see No. 10). Notice the texture of everything you handle and each texture with which you come in contact – glass, timber, metal, cloth, liquid etc.

23. Self-pleasuring

(BAOYB&J) By the term 'self pleasuring', I don't necessarily mean in a sexual sense, although this is an extremely important aspect of our interactions with the world around us. Adopt a childlike fascination with your senses and make mental notes (or physical ones if it helps) of the sensations that give you the most pleasure. Run your fingers and hands over every inch of your body and note the areas that are most appreciative of gentle caresses and the areas that react favourably to more forceful kneading and massaging. As infants and children we would have once spent hours unashamedly exploring our bodily sensations. Many of us spend months and even years waiting for someone to touch us in a way that makes us feel valued or cared for. Most of these sensations we crave can be self-accessed, if only we have the courage to explore our need for giving and receiving pleasure. Once we know our own physical likes and dislikes, we can then instruct our partners in the art of pleasing us. (BAOYB&J)

24. Receiving a Massage

As part of learning how to receive a massage it is important to know exactly which sensations are most pleasing to us. (see No. 23) With this information we can guide our masseur/masseuse to give us the type of massage we either want or need.

Begin by noticing how you feel about removing your clothes and laying on the massage table (or chair). Feel the texture of the table covering under you and the towel or sheet over you. (BAOYB&J) Notice the temperature of the hands on your body and the texture of their skin. Is the massage oil, cream or powder cool, or has it been pre-heated? In your mind, follow the hands as they stroke, knead, squeeze and pummel. Follow them as they move from one section of your body to another. (BAOYB&J) Make mental notes of the areas that need the most attention and make a conscious effort to relax that spot and allow the blood flow to heal or ease the discomfort. As each area is completed be aware of any tingling sensation as the blood flows in to restore and renew.

At the end of the massage, try to allow enough time to fully experience the effect of gravity pushing you onto the table and the lack of tension in your muscles.

25. Giving a Massage

As you place your hands on the body you are about to massage, try to synchronise your breathing with theirs. If it is fast, make a mental note to slow down your own and theirs will probably follow suit. Feel the texture of the oil as you apply it to your hands. (BAOYB&J) Notice how the skin of the body you are massaging moves under your hands and how it springs back to its original place when they have passed. Feel the temperature of the body and note the amount of hair that is present. Notice any tendency to judge aspects of the body you are touching. Is there any fragrance in the oil? As you breathe in, become aware of the path of your breath through your nose, down your throat and into your diaphragm and lungs. Try to co-ordinate your breathing with the movements of your hands, keeping them both flowing and rhythmical. As you lift the recipient's arms and legs, notice if they are holding any tension in their muscles. If you lift their foot off the table, assess if you feel it would stay there if you let it go? Experiment with the amount of pressure you apply, while always being aware of the needs of the recipient. Alternate from light flowing strokes to heavier percussive movements and be aware of the sensations in your own hands as you do this. At the end of the massage,

leave your hands resting lightly on the recipient, feeling their body temperature, noting their rate of breathing and yours, and feeling any heat or energy transferring between you. (BAOYB&J)

26. Toilets

I know that in most cultures this is a subject seldom discussed, except maybe in hospitals where talk of 'bowel movements' and 'urine samples' is often elevated to the status of major topics. (BAOYB&J) But when you consider that there are few activities more regular in our daily routines than our trips to the 'John', or 'the loo' or 'the can' (or any one of a hundred other euphemisms), then I believe that these brief interruptions to our activities lend themselves ideally to the Self Observation scenario. (BAOYB&J) You may be pleased to know that I'm not going to go into graphic descriptions of what to look out for, except to warn you to be aware, as with all the other scripts, of all your senses. Be especially careful not to judge any part of you anatomy or any of your natural bodily functions. This particular observation can be a fantastic lesson in acceptance. Believe me, we would be in dire straits if this facet of our humanness ceased to function! (BAOYB&J)

27. Vacuuming (or 'Hoovering' in the UK)

(BAOYB&J) Feel the texture and temperature of the hose and tubing in your hand. Feel the weight of the machine as you drag or wheel it, or it trails along behind you. Listen to the unique sound the motor makes and the subtle changes in pitch as it slides over a different surface or picks up something. Notice the positioning of your feet as you work and feel the muscles propel you back and forth as you manipulate the vacuuming head across the floor. Be aware of the movement of your arms and the tightening muscles in your back as you lean forward with each forward thrust and try to identify which muscles operate to bring you back into an upright position. Can you notice a difference in the way the pile lays after you have vacuumed it? What can you smell in the air? Is there a dusty odour? No judgement here – not good or bad, but just the way it is. (BAOYB&J)

Mantras and Chanting

Mantra is a word so new to the English language that it still has not made its way into all dictionaries. It has however been part of the

Eastern vocabulary for thousands of years. It can be most simply described as a word, phrase or short sentence, which may or may not (depending on which school of thought you follow) have meaning. The most common of them contain references to a deity or spiritual aim. One of the most well known mantras in western society, especially since the 1960's, was made famous by the Hare Krishna movement.

> Hare Krishna, Hare Krishna, Krishna, Krishna, Hare Hare
> Hare Rama, Hare Rama, Krishna, Krishna, Hare Hare

I have heard numerous different, longer and shorter versions in my travels, but basically they all amount to a continual repetition of an expression of a love of God. It is generally believed that continual chanting of the various names of the chosen deity will bring the chanter closer to God and spiritual enlightenment. (BAOYB&J)

Of course there are also physical, psychological and physiological benefits of musical and rhythmical chanting, the most important being – it just feels good. The body loves rhythm and music. In its most simple form, chanting mantras is a way of creating the same physiological sensations attributed to the playing of music. It has a way of calming the nervous system and relieving tension. If performed simultaneously with others it can have a profound effect on physical and psychological well-being. (See chapter on Belonging) (BAOYB&J)

28. Om mani padme hungm (or Aum Marni Padmay Hung)

This is a Buddhist chant. The closest I have been able to get to a direct translation of this is: 'There is a spark in all of us which is precious and it is this spark that connects us to all other living things and the universe.'

My personal experience of this chant has been that it sets up a vibration through my whole body that leaves me tingling and relaxed when I stop. (BAOYB&J)

29. Self-Composed Chants

Try it. Piece together a set of words, sounds (they don't even have to make sense) or phrases that create a rhythm or sound that makes you

feel good. (BAOYB&J) The word 'Calm – ing' is quite popular or 'Re
– lax', coordinated with the rhythm of the breath.

30. Sound or Rhythm Chants

Try the vowel sounds: A - E - I - O - U, one at a time and with a separate breath for each. This is a great one to practise with other people
who sing the notes in harmony. Very cool! If you don't feel confident
about being able to emit a distinct tone, then try making rhythmical
noises, either with your mouth… or your hands… or knocking your
knees together… It's a bit like using the hypnotic rhythm of drum-
ming… without the drums. Or playing the spoons… without spoons.

Object Focus

Unlike scripts 1-27, which invite you to focus on all aspects of your
immediate environment, Object Focus is as it suggests, focussed on
one point alone. One hundred percent of your attention is channelled
to a chosen spot, the objective being to centre all attention so
intensely that anything outside your focus zone simply doesn't exist
in your consciousness.

31. Stream

An environmental observation by a stream can be a very rewarding
experience, but the stream (or ocean waves / clouds) can make a
great object focussed observation on its own. You might choose to
alternate between a broad environmental observation and a point-
focused observation. It really is entirely up to you.

(BAOYB&J) Hear the various sounds that the water makes as it flows
around and collides with the rocks or branches or sand. You could
focus on an overview of sounds or even just one sound for this observation. Or maybe you would like to focus on just one tiny patch of
water or mini waterfall. Notice the way the light catches each droplet
as it is flung forward or splashes back form an obstacle. You could
choose the cool, moist air as the subject and notice how this air enters
your nose and fills and nourishes your lungs and your body.

As with all the observation scripts,
experiment to find what works for you.

32. Sunrise/Sunset

Similar to No. 31 – the Stream. Start with a general broad observation then focus in on the effect the sunset/rise has on the light surrounding the scene. Notice the changing colours of the sky – and the variety of colours – and how each cloud is effected by the movement of the sun (or earth if you want to be more scientifically correct) Be aware of the change in intensity of the light and how the sharpness of the shadows indicates this change. (BAOYB&J) Is there a change in temperature as the sun rises or sets and how does this make you feel? Experiment with breathing in the different colours and observe the effect that has on you emotionally or mentally. Do some colours lift you up while others influence you to be sad or thoughtful? (BAOYB&J)

33. Candle

While focussing on the flame, become aware of all the different colours that are visible in such a small area. (BAOYB&J) Notice the fuzzy gold tip of the flame and how the intensity softens as it nears the wick. The tip of the wick usually glows with a deep red that gradually fades into the blackness lower down. Is the flame completely still or does it bend and sway with each tiny movement of air. Choose one spot on the flame and feel your eyes penetrating that point. Breathe the warmth of the flame deep into your body and feel the cooler air flow from your nose or mouth as you exhale. Each time your mind drifts away from your chosen point of focus, gently coax it back and notice how your breath calms and settles into a gentle rhythm that matches the sway and flicker of the flame. Try to imagine that you are in the centre of the flame – become part of it.

Visualisations

To visualise is merely to imagine or create a mental picture of something, which is actually what we all do, all day, in every waking moment (and even in the non-waking ones). We do not think in words, we see in pictures. When we're about to descend a flight of stairs, our minds do not picture the word 'stairs', but instead, our eyes fix on the first five or six steps, mentally photograph them, and while talking to our companion or remembering last night's movie, we casually walk down the visual image we have created of the stairs. We very rarely set our eyes on each step as we go down. Think about it. (BAOYB&J)

Visualising is something we all do naturally, but often without realising it. When we talk on the phone we will usually have some sort of mental picture of either the person we are talking to or the subject we are discussing. And especially for those of you who claim to have trouble visualising, imagine I was talking to you on the telephone and just happened to mention that I'd seen an elephant. I challenge you not to see an elephant! Don't picture it! Don't see it's long trunk it's massive legs and it's huge floppy ears! How did you do?

We also visualise constantly when we are simply moving about doing our daily chores. While you are reading this book you already have a mental image of your surroundings. To test this, close your eyes at the end of this sentence and look at the image of your surroundings which is etched into your memory. We can use this faculty positively or negatively. I think we have all experienced a mental argument with someone, minutes or even hours before we are due to see them. This is all apart of the *expectation* process. And do you realise that what you see is really only an 'image' of reality projected through the lens (cornea) and onto the screen (retina) at the back of your eye? What you are seeing now is in fact the result of light reflected from objects into your eyes, which is converted into electrical impulses which part of your brain interprets as visual information. In short, all you see is actually an *illusion*.

So, to put your illusions to work for you, you can imagine or visualise images that aid your meditative or relaxation process. The scope is as wide and vivid as your imagination, but I have listed a few possibilities gleaned from friends, colleagues and students, as well as from my own private collection. (BAOYB&J)

34. Flying

(BAOYB&J) Of course if you have ever travelled anywhere on a plane you will be aware that the whole process of flying begins days earlier than the actual flight – calling your travel agent, sorting itineraries, buying the ticket, packing your suitcases. As with the rest of your life, any of these scenarios will make a perfect subject for self-observation, but for the moment I would like to focus on the stages beginning with actually boarding the aircraft. If you are a nervous flyer then complete focus on the activities of the present moment will prevent you dwelling on the 'might happens' in the near future.

How do you feel as you walk down the gangway toward the open door and the waiting flight crew? What physical sensations do you experience as you settle into your seat and fasten your seat belt? Are you excited or a little nervous? Listen to the sounds of the other passengers finding their seats, stowing their hand luggage and fastening their seat belts. What other noises can you hear? (BAOYB&J) Can you hear the clatter and thump of the cargo holds under the floor; the whine of the jet engines as they idle before take-off; the soft hum of the air conditioning? Feel the texture of the seating and the arm rests; the vibration of things being loaded onto the plane and then the slight rocking movements as the aircraft begins to taxi toward the runway. Make sure you focus on all the safety announcements and emergency procedures. (BAOYB&J) As the plane turns onto the runway, listen to the change in pitch of the engines as they increase power; feel the thrust of acceleration force you back into your seat as it gathers speed; feel the upward motion as the aircraft finally gains sufficient velocity to leave the ground and listen for the sound of the landing gear folding into the underbelly. Marvel at the technology that enables you to sit in a metal tube and in relative comfort, hurtling through the air at six hundred miles per hour and at 35000 feet where the outside temperature is around minus 50 degrees. Doesn't it strike you as being just a little bit surreal?

35. Gaining altitude (shrinking your problems)

This is one that I remember teaching to my children when they were quite young. It is great for looking objectively at your problems and seeing them for what they usually are – trivial.

(BAOYB&J) Imagine yourself standing with your problem. It may be an object, a project, a person or an event – but just see yourself being physically close to this situation. Let's say it is a conflict situation you are having with another person. Imagine you are standing with them and looking into their eyes. Try to feel what you feel when you are actually with this person. (BAOYB&J)

Now imagine you are suspended form the ceiling but looking down on the scene i.e. you can see both you and the other person and you are looking down on the top of their heads from about 10 feet in the air. For the next step you may need to exercise your imagination a little further than you are used to. Imagine that the ceiling and the roof are transparent and you are floating above the building. You can see the entire building and still see the two people in their conflict. Next, see yourself soaring to a height of three or four hundred feet so that you can see the whole block of houses in your area and you can just barely make out the two figures through the transparent roof. Up you go still further until you can see the entire county... and still further until you can see three or four counties or a whole state... and still further until you can see the whole country... then half the planet... the whole planet... and then to a point where the continents become indistinct and planet earth becomes a pretty blue ball in an endless universe...and now find your problem. (BAOYB&J)

What if problems were only as large or as small as the amount of energy we chose to allot them? When people say 'Oh my God! What a nightmare!' I say, 'Compared to what?' We constantly need to look carefully at the size of our problems relative to the amount of energy we are willing to spend on them.

36. Beach walking

As someone born in Australia and now living in England, I sometimes find myself pining for sunshine and long golden beaches. When this happens, I just combine the stored images I have of hundreds of trips to the beach and I recreate my ideal beach scene. (BAOYB&J)

Transport yourself to any stored beach scene memory. Feel the sand between your toes and the crunch or squeak as the underside of your foot makes contact with it. As you approach the harder sand near the waters edge, notice the different feel it has on the skin of the soles of your feet. Feel the sensation of the water on your feet – is it warm or cold? Feel the clothes against your body (if you are wearing any. It's your visualisation – you don't have to wear clothes if you don't want to) If you are wearing clothes, feel them rubbing against your body as you walk or the breeze pushing them against your skin. Can you feel the warmth of the sun? Breath in that warmth and feel the fresh salty tang as it is drawn deep into your lungs. If you decide to go for a swim, feel the coolness of the water on your legs as you wade into the shallows, up to your waist and then tingling over your whole body as you plunge into the waves. (BAOYB&J)

There is a variation I like to add to my beach visualisation. I picture myself running along the beach, faster and faster, until I lift off the sand and begin to fly, gliding silently along the tops of the waves like a seagull and then flying high above the sand dunes. I can experience the exhilaration of soaring around rocky headlands on the warm updrafts generated by the hot dunes, or skimming over a tranquil ocean like an albatross. I find the freedom extremely relaxing.

37. Erotica

(BAOYB&J) There's probably no need to go into graphic descriptions or erotic scenarios here; they can be acquired from any number of sources if required. The important thing for us to realise is that most of our sexual enjoyment is dependent on our mental capabilities, not our physical ones. How many of our actual sexual experiences really equate to the perfect scenarios we concoct in our heads? In our minds we can romp naked with the partner of our dreams and completely devoid of guilt or fear. Imagined lovers don't have unrealistic expectations of us, make selfish demands or need us to call them the next day. I'm not suggesting that they can completely replace our physical counterparts, but in the realms of my imagination, the partner I have can be the partner I want. (BAOYB&J)

38. Travelling

Mental itineraries can be cobbled together using replayed, real-life journeys; images from movies, documentaries or travel shows; totally imaginary scenes and places; or a mixture of all three. (BAOYB&J) One of my personal favourites is to imagine I am riding in the First Class dining car of a 1920's style luxury European train. The table is set on white linen, the cutlery silver, the crockery is fine bone china, the food superb and the wine is rich, full bodied and usually French or Australian. We are chugging sedately through the Swiss Alps… or the Canadian Rockies… or the frozen wastes of Siberia… I simply change the view out the window depending on my current mood or desires.

39. Favourite places and times

(BAOYB&J) This can be done in a thousand different ways. I generally start by picturing myself in orbit around the planet. As I pass over a country, I picture a place in that country where I had a pleasant experience. At one moment I can zoom in on the Eiffel Tower in Paris and enjoy the view over the Seine toward the Trocadero. In another instant I can be sitting at a restaurant table in Sorrento on the Amalfi Coast of Italy. For dessert I can be with friends around a campfire outside a log cabin in the highlands of Tasmania, and just as suddenly I am sleeping under a canopy of stars in the Great Australian Desert. It is a way of cementing and storing what I call the *Golden Moments* of my life, and they can include everything from the birth of my children to the last time I sat and drank beer with my father. It's all there, good times and interesting times, all to be viewed again at will and all teaching me something about myself and this complicated tale I call my life. (BAOYB&J)

40. Golden Ball of Energy

This is also called Zone Relaxation, in reference to the different zones of the body you can focus on. It is best done when you can lie on a floor or a bed, but can be modified to work in a chair. You can also use it as a script for another person to read and talk you through this process.

Lay with your eyes closed and arms by your side and legs comfortably together. Placing a pillow under your knees will make you more com-fortable, particularly if you have lower back trouble. Check your breathing to make sure it is reasonably slow and deep before you start. (BAOYB&J)

Focus your attention on your toes and imagine that, hovering just above them is a fuzzy ball of energy, like a tiny, glowing golden haystack – about the size of a football. Feel the warmth emanating from this fuzzy ball and imagine it settling down to rest on the tops of your toes. In your mind, see it divide into two and simultaneously the two balls begin to enter your body through your toes and travel down slowly through your feet toward your heels. As they pass through your skin, muscles and bones you can feel them soaking up any tension that you have stored in those tissues and leaving behind a tingling, warm and relaxed feeling. They keep moving, passing through your ankles and begin the journey up your legs. Feel the ten-sion being soaked up as they travel through your calf muscles and up to your knees. Slowly they move upwards and you notice that with every in-breath they move a little further up your body. Passing through your thighs now and toward your hip bones, joining back together in your groin area, the two fuzzy balls of energy become one wide ribbon and begin to move along your torso. It is removing all the tension from your stomach and lower back, now your midriff and mid back, up into your chest and upper back and eventually to your collarbones and shoulders. Let them rest here for a moment while you scan your body from your toes up to your shoulders and experience the warm, buzzing sensation of complete relaxation. (BAOYB&J)

The large golden ball divides again as one small ball travels down each arm to the tips of your fingers, and then they begin the slow journey, drawn by each in-breath, through your fingers, hands, wrists, forearms, elbows, upper arms, shoulders – and then they join together again as the large ball travels into your throat and neck. Feel the skin and muscles relax as with each breath the energy seeps into your jaw and face, the back of your neck, your nose, eyes, forehead, back of your head and finally drawn out through your crown by what seems like an invisible magnetic force. The fuzzy, golden ball of energy then draws away from you and disappears, taking with it all the tension from your body. (BAOYB&J)

Scan your body one more time and enjoy the feeling of complete relaxation for a few minutes before either getting up, or perhaps going off to sleep.

41. Mountain Trail

(BAOYB&J) This can be as vivid, exciting, relaxing or as far ranging as your imagination can create. Picture yourself walking along a mountain trail. Beside you, to the right, is a drop of several hundred feet to a river below. On the left is a rock wall that soars to a height several thousand feet above you and terminates in a snow-capped peak silhouetted against a vivid blue sky. The track is narrow and rocky and winds casually along a narrow ledge. Up ahead you can see a suspension bridge that spans the river gorge at a narrow point and links with a similar trail along a cliff wall on the other side of the ravine. The crossing draws closer and closer with every step and you can feel your heartbeat start to quicken at the prospect of having to traverse a gently swaying cable bridge, hundreds of feet above an icy mountain stream. Finally you are there, standing on the uneven gravel approach to the aging and rickety structure. Tentatively you take your first step onto the weathered timber slats that make up the flooring of the footway. You now have both feet on the bridge, hands clinging tightly to the wire handrails on each side. Every step is greeted with a return bounce from the spring in the cables and there is an unsettling swing as you approach the centre of the bridge. You are at the half way point now, and looking down you notice that there are several slats missing just ahead. A three foot yawning gap exposes a dizzying view to the river far below, but there is no going back – you need to get to the other side. Taking a deep breath, you grip either side of the cable handrails and swing your body over the gap, landing gently on the other side. Waiting a moment for the resultant swaying to subside, you briefly glance back at the trail and the section of bridge your have just traversed, and then turn to go on your way... (Continue wherever your imagination takes you) (BAOYB&J)

42. Sailing

(BAOYB&J) Combine all your knowledge of sailing and the sea to include anything that will quicken or slow your heart rate. It really doesn't matter how much real life sailing experience you have. Years of exposure to movies and television, or even sitting on a headland watching the boats go by, will have given you enough mental images to create your own sailing scenario. If it is adventure you are after, imagine you are riding through the storms and mountainous seas of Cape Horn. (BAOYB&J) If relaxation is more to your liking, picture yourself lolling on the deck of a catamaran in the calm waters of the Mediterranean. It's your call.

43. Healing

More and more the power of the mind is being recognised as a major tool for the healing of our bodies. (BAOYB&J) Our thoughts are responsible for triggering all sorts of chemical responses in our bodies, so why should we be surprised that we can use this facility to our advantage. The method is the same for most ailments and involves the brain sending mental i.e. electrical signals, to any part of the body we choose. Positive messages and mental visions of health accelerate the healing process. Numerous comments from doctors around the world confirm that the most important mental life-saving tool for any human being is their will to live. Survival is much more probable in any given medical prognosis if the patient can hold a clear image of their health on the other side of the illness.

The basic procedure:

Close your eyes, monitor your breathing for a minute or two, and get a mental image of your heart slowing down and pumping calmly and rhythmically. Focus now on the area that is painful or requires healing. If it is painful (a headache or back ache perhaps) allot a value out of ten to the intensity of the pain. If a value of 1 is barely noticeable, and 10 is excruciating, where on this scale does this pain sit? See the size, shape, colour, consistency and texture of the area you want to reduce or change. How long and how wide is this shape? Is it round, square, rectangular? Attempt to describe the shape in words. Now give it an exact measurement in inches or centimetres – exactly how wide / long is it? What colour is it and how saturated is that colour i.e. Is it a deep blue or a light blue? Is it hard like metal, softer and more brittle like wood, or softer again like rubber or spongy like marshmallow? Is the texture rough like course sandpaper or smooth like glass? (BAOYB&J)

Once you have completed this cycle, start again. What intensity is the pain now? (between 1 and 10) Has it reduced? And what size is it now? Smaller? And so on… Repeat this several times, or as long as you feel you are getting positive results. As with any of these visualisations, it often works better if someone talks you through it or asks you the questions. (BAOYB&J)

For Couples

44. Eye to Eye

(BAOYB&J) Focus on the eyes of your partner as if you are using them for an Object Focussed observation. Spoken communication seems almost unnecessary after 20 minutes or so of this type of intense contact. Also works well when combined with the following observation.

45. Synchronised Breathing

Sit or stand facing each other with one hand placed in the centre of each other's chest, just below the collarbones. Start with your eyes closed and try to match the rhythm of your breathing with theirs. The hand on the chest will help you ascertain the rhythm of your partner's breathing and after several minutes you will usually find that you will both slip into a synchronised breathing pattern. It is a very useful technique for establishing common ground, especially when

normal methods of communication seem to be breaking down. (BAOYB&J)

46. Massage

Follow the instructions as for individual observations on giving and receiving massages. (No. 24 and No. 25) (BAOYB&J) Do it simultaneously and at all times be aware of the needs of your partner as well as your own. Imagine if this could be achieved in every aspect of your relationship. If you don't have the time or the space for a full body massage, a mutual foot massage on the sofa can be very rewarding.

47. Mutual Mastication

Follow the script for the Eating observation (No. 10) and as with Number 46, above, take the needs of your partner into account. (BAOYB&J) Have a plate each, or one shared plate, with bite size chunks of your favourite foods. Use a fork if you must, but I find it a much more sensual experience to feed your partner, using your fingers to pick up the food and place it gently in their mouth. Take your time and garnish the meal with plenty of eye contact.

48. Singing or chanting

Revisit the section on Mantras and Chanting (before No. 28) and then practice blending your chants. (BAOYB&J) If you find it too difficult to harmonise your mantras, just try singing together or chanting to the same rhythm. Echo chants can also work well with one following the other to create a rhythmical pattern. Have fun with it – play and experiment. If you're not enjoying it, try something else. There are as many ways of blending talents as there are people in this world.

49. Dancing

(BAOYB&J) Practise in the privacy of your own home to be fully conversant with your own body movements and how they blend with those of your partner. As with the synchronised breathing, practice moving and responding to each of your partner's movements until you flow with each other. Like professional ice skaters, it is possible, with sufficient practice and patience to reach a point where your bodies move as one – i.e. not obvious to those watching where one starts and the other stops.

50. Making Love (or Sexual Intercourse... or whatever you call it in your part of the world)

(BAOYB&J) No instructions really needed here. Using all the tools mentioned so far for creating awareness, heighten all your senses to fully appreciate and be totally involved with creating pleasure for yourself and for each other. Focus on each of your senses in turn or in a delicious overview. Maintain focus so as to be 100% present with your partner in this most intimate form of communication.

And in **YOUR** life...

As this is already a whole chapter about observing *your* life, it seems a bit pointless adding more practice here. My only extra suggestion would be to encourage you to use every moment of every day as an opportunity to learn more about yourself and your world.

OBSERVATION SCRIPTS

IN THIRTY WORDS OR LESS...

'We often rush through the moment to get to the joy. If we choose to stop and fully experience the moment we will find the joy is already present.'

My friend, colleague and teacher, Dr Hilda Des Arts,
who inspired me with her meaning of life:
to 'Live, love, learn and leave a legacy'.

CHAPTER NINE

CREATING STRESS

It's an inside job

Primarily this is a book about creating what we want, but it will probably be useful to discuss how we go about creating what we don't want and the affect that has on our lives. For example – anger, sadness, discomfort or any of those undesirable feelings that we would rather not create. Notice I didn't say *avoid*. *Not creating* situations where we experience these emotions is not the same as avoiding them once they have been created. Avoidance is tantamount to sweeping it under the carpet. Unless we face the issue, it will probably reappear somewhere else in our lives, perhaps under a different heading. Resentment left un-aired can fester into anger and then possibly to violence, at others or ourselves.

Acknowledging that we have the power to create the things in our lives that we don't want, automatically implies that we have the power to un-create them, or better still, to create the things that we do want instead. What a concept! Maybe for the sake of simplicity we can give the label of *Stress* to all those displeasing and uncomfortable reactions we experience when confronting a challenging situation. Stress is a name for something we find it difficult to define. But lets imagine that stress occurs for us when we create results that are directly in conflict with our original intention or plan.

I intend to have a peaceful day relaxing and I create tension by choosing to go shopping instead. I intend to sit calmly with my wife over dinner and then I choose to create conflict over the choice of wine. I intend to give feedback to my staff member and I create a situation where he wants to resign. I intend to create trophies and cash and I end up with a wooden spoon and an empty wallet.

Of course these things can be stressful, but maybe they came about because I wasn't sufficiently clear about my intention in the first place. We love to analyse why things didn't work out for us and how upset we felt at the time. Perhaps the greatest challenge facing us is how we learn to see stress as something we create. With this in mind

we can observe ourselves creating stress, become aware of the details of that creation process, and translate those awarenesses into tools for creating what we do want. If we accept that we are the active participants in creating stress, then it is only a short journey to the point where we accept that we can also create its antidote – success. But that comes a little further down the track. For now let's talk about:

What is stress?

When some thing or system is designed to carry a certain load, or perform a set of functions, and that load is exceeded, then it is said to be 'under stress'.

EXAMPLE:
    a)   10-ton truck on bridge with 5-ton load limit

    b)   Retail outlet, staffed to receive 1000 customers, is stampeded by 2000 customers.

OR   A thing or system receives a *normal* load (whatever that is) but the thing or system is flawed, weakened or malfunctioning, or perhaps not being used for that which it was designed.

EXAMPLE:
    a)   Design fault or use of lower quality material

    b)   Using a fork as a corkscrew, screwdriver as a tyre lever, or your hand as a hammer.

Main causes of human stress

1 Living an unbalanced life (weakening the system)

Solution: Balance the Physical / Mental / Emotional and Spiritual aspects of your life. It's a lot like caring for your car. You can tune it, polish it, vacuum the interior and fill it with high performance fuel, but if the tyres are flat it will still run terribly! – See chapter on LIFESTYLE MATTERS.

2 Taking on too much (overloading)

Solution: Learn to say 'No!' Listen to the voice of intuition that says, 'Are you sure this a good idea? Are you wanting to say 'yes', to please someone else? What's best for YOU?'

3 Taking on tasks for which we aren't suited (not designed for)

Solution: Be aware of your own strengths and weaknesses and choose tasks accordingly. If you still need to attempt a project with which you are not entirely comfortable, at least be aware of the expectations you may have around the outcome you want to produce.

In other words, stress has more to do with the *thought* than the event. And it has much more to do with reliving past events and projecting fears into the future than it does with the present moment.

Is it all an illusion?

Let's play the 'What if…' game again. Let's suspend judgement and analysis for a moment and explore the possible existence of a concept we may not have previously considered.

What if stress is just a nasty little game my mind plays on me, and then my body tags along for the ride? What would happen if I could change the way I look at situations and people instead of trying to change the actual situations and people themselves? What if the problems in my life were only as large or small as the amount of energy I chose to allot them?

If you have ever read any books or articles on lifestyle, attended lectures on health or have even half listened to the news broadcasts and advertising with which we are constantly bombarded, you will have noticed how often the word *stress* turns up in regard to health issues. It seems that science and the medical profession have finally caught up with something that most of us have known for years. i.e. Constant worrying and anxiety reduces our chances of remaining healthy. So…what are we stressing about?

Once upon a time the word 'stress' was worn like a badge of importance and it's contemporaries were words like 'deadline', 'meeting' and 'mobile phone'. But in these days of equality and political correctness, stress has become non-discriminatory – anyone can have it, brag about it and suffer from it – but more importantly, anyone can learn how to manage it.

Do we need stress?

The survival of our Neanderthal ancestors relied in no small part on the ability of their bodies to respond quickly to physical danger. When set upon by a sabre-tooth tiger, the hypothalamus, pituitary gland and adrenal gland all joined forces to shut down non-essential services (stomach, spleen, immune system etc) and direct blood supply to the major muscle groups to facilitate a speedy exit (flight) or an heroic stand (fight). When the immediate danger had passed, all systems returned to normal in a relatively short space of time. And when danger threatens us, this same ancient and primitive (and amazingly sophisticated) system cranks up to afford us the protection we need.

So, is stress useful? Yes! It can save our lives!

But in our relatively safe suburban environment do we perhaps call on our safety system a little unnecessarily? Stress can certainly arouse our self-protection mechanisms, but how much is too much?

> '...up to a point, arousal can improve our performance on a task, but beyond that point performance will tend to decline. If we are too aroused, whether by fear, anger, happiness (or lust), we are unlikely to be able to do our best possible work; the optimal level of arousal is not the same as the highest level.'
> YERKES-DODSON LAW - THE RELATIONSHIP BETWEEN PERFORMANCE AND AROUSAL.' PSYCHOLOGY – AN INTRODUCTION.

I don't know about you, but it seems as if it's been some time since I – or any of my relatives and friends – have been threatened by a sabre-tooth tiger, but my nervous system still keeps in practice. Stress attacks, often accompanied by fist clenching, waste bin kicking and screaming of profanities, are more often triggered by such life threatening events as... missing my train, encountering a rude shop assistant or, heaven forbid, someone borrowing my favourite pen without asking me first!

If there is a constant flow of these irritating little events in our day, and we automatically launch into the *fight or flight* response, our bodies don't have sufficient time to settle back to normal. Our pulse rates remain high, the adrenal system is constantly pouring high-octane fuel into our bloodstream and our minds retain that hormone (drug) induced sharpness, keeping us prepared for the next perceived calamity. Is it any wonder we return home feeling exhausted but still find it difficult to relax? Somewhere along the evolutionary trail, probably because of a drastically reduced number of physical threats in our day to day environment, we have elevated a whole range of trivial items to the top half of our list of perceived dangers. Logically progressing along this line of thinking, it becomes obvious that stress is not a direct result of an event, but totally governed by our perception of that event.

A simple solution

'Life is simple. Why do men and women seek to make it complicated?'
CONFUCIUS

The ideas and concepts presented here are not new. The models and anecdotes I use to define and highlight them might be, but the concepts themselves are old and the basic principles are embarrassingly simple. By a strange and paradoxical process the fastest route to understanding, in a useful and practical sense, is through the abandonment of the need to understand. In other words, true understanding will come when we understand that the complexities of body, mind, spirit, the universe and relationships (have I missed anything?) are all far too complex to ever completely understand.

For example, how many people do you know who can give a clear, concise and accurate scientific explanation of the theory of gravity? Not many? Well what about a simple, layman's outline of the day-to-day effects of gravity? How about, 'What goes up, must come down?' Won't this get us through most of life's eventualities? Maybe the answers to our questions on stress are just as simple.

And as another example… Do you know how to use a ballpoint pen? Yes? Then, would it be any more useful an instrument if you knew the molecular formation or atomic structure of the materials involved in the construction of a ballpoint pen? Does not knowing these things stop you from writing with one?

I wake in the middle of the night to hear strange noises and footsteps in my house. I am terrified. I have to know who or what it is and if I am in danger. Can you imagine it? I lean to one side of my bed, reach to turn the light on but then… suddenly, I stop. Frozen with fear and disappointment I burst into tears and scream, 'It's no use! I can't use

the switch because I don't understand electricity!'

Perhaps we don't need to know every minute detail of an issue or problem to be effective at handling it. Maybe we don't need to understand before we act. Sure, you will be able to come up with copious quantities of examples where detailed analysis is imperative. Reading the finer details of a contract, or at least finding someone who can, may be one. And a scientist would need to have an expectation of a possible result, based on careful analysis and experiment, before combining two or more volatile substances. But on the whole, in our average, domestic, work-a-day lives, the trick is to get far enough away from something to see its simplicity. Held up close to our noses, even the most trivial irritation can look enormous, while holding it at a distance can evoke objectivity and a shift in our perception. Our favourite teachers are usually the ones who are most adept at highlighting the essence of a situation, reducing it to it's basic components and then helping us to relate to it by way of analogy, metaphor or comparison with something with which we already have a fair grasp.

We can use this objectivity to simplify our picture of the world we inhabit. We can then use this picture to create situations that please us, therefore reducing the incidence of situations that stress us. There really is a simple solution.

And in <u>YOUR</u> life...

1. Identify a recent time when you felt stressed about a minor incident e.g. spilt your coffee, missed your train or forgot to take out the garbage. What was your expectation before the event – that you wouldn't spill the coffee? Could you have had a more realistic expectation? e.g. 'The combination of the effects of gravity and your imperfect physical co-ordination makes occasional spillage highly probable.'

    Could you have changed the event? Possibly, with extra care. In any case, it will probably make you more cautious in the future. E.g. Hold tighter, walk slower, watch out for obstacles.

    What was you evaluation of the event? e.g. That you are a clumsy fool and should not be trusted with milk ever again? How could you have adjusted your evaluation of the event? e.g. 'It is unreasonable to expect that I will not make errors of judgement. I will clean up the mess and endeavour to learn from the experience. I just got a free lesson.'

Now try the above process on the major events of your life – past, present and future.

2. How do you weaken your own system? In broad terms, what do you do that reduces your capacity for coping with stress? (The next chapter will assist you to identify actual and potential trouble spots.)

3. In which areas of your life could you be more assertive and say 'No!' more often?

4. Are you playing to your strengths? How could you do more of what you enjoy and are good at and less of what causes you to feel stressed.

5. Self observation will enhance your ability to be more objective. Train yourself to notice when you begin to feel the symptoms of stress e.g. heart pounding, palms sweating, a general feeling of unease. Identify the thoughts that led to these symptoms. i.e. your thoughts surrounding your expectations, the event and the evaluation. How could you re-evaluate your thoughts to trigger a hit of feel good chemicals?

CREATING STRESS

IN THIRTY WORDS OR LESS...

'Just as we use the power of expectation to create the life we want, if we are not careful, we will create the sort of stressed life we don't want.'

You are what you **EAT!**
…and what you **DO!**
…and what you **THINK!**
…and what you **FEEL!**
…and what you **BELIEVE!**

CHAPTER TEN

LIFESTYLE MATTERS

Creating a healthy, satisfying and fulfilling lifestyle for myself is dependent on much more than awareness, expectation and monitoring my thought processes. Before I can commence getting my physical health in order, I need to have a reason or motivation to keep me on target. The *why* is more important than the *how* because without an *inspiring why*, I am never going to get a *committed how*.

Without going into loads of technical guff about the benefits of exercising and eating healthy food – which we've all heard a thousand times anyway and most of us believe – it is probably enough to remind ourselves that, when we feel good, we usually do good – or even if we don't do good then at least we haven't got the added burden of feeling bad on top of not doing good!

The Holistic Wheel of Health

One of the simple models I use in workshops and private life coaching, to demonstrate the need for balance in our lives, is a diagram I call *The Holistic Wheel of Health*. I have presented it in health resorts, corporate training programmes and to people of all ages and backgrounds. The overwhelming response has been one of amazement at its simplicity and power as a tool for stimulating lifestyle awareness.

To personalise the next phase of our discussion, I suggest that you follow the instructions carefully to build your own Wheel of Health. The insights you gain will provide useful background information for the creation of ideas to balance your life.

Creating your own Holistic Wheel of Health

On the following pages you will find a framework and instructions for constructing and balancing your wheel. The term 'holistic' refers to the fact that it attempts to cover all aspects of our lives.

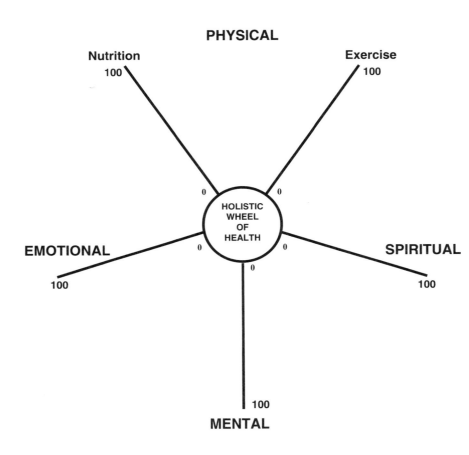

You are what you **EAT!**

…and what you **DO!**

…and what you **THINK!**

…and what you **FEEL!**

…and what you **BELIEVE!**

Figure 3

The wheel is designed to cover the four pillars of health:

- Physical
- Emotional
- Mental
- Spiritual

The Emotional, Mental and Spiritual aspects are each allotted their own spoke and dividing the Physical aspect into Nutrition and Exercise creates the fourth and fifth spokes. Begin by placing a mark on each spoke of the wheel, somewhere between 0 and 100, in relation to how you rate your performance in that particular aspect of your life, taking an average over the last 3 months. If that sounds complex, don't worry; I will talk you through each stage. Let's start with one of the two physical aspects.

Exercise Spoke

If 100 represents your optimum exercise quota for the week – say, three one hour sessions at the gym and a couple of long walks on the weekend – and 0 represents complete couch potato-ness with no exercise at all; where do you place yourself on this scale? And while we're on the subject, did you know that exercise does much more for you than just build muscle and burn calories? Just one solid half hour workout that gets your heart pumping and makes you raise a sweat will elevate your metabolic rate for up to 40 hours giving your whole system a workout and improving the efficiency of your bodily functions. It will also give you an extra squirt of endorphin to increase your 'feel good' quota and this overflows into everything else you tackle, improving performance, which increases your 'feel good' quota...and so on.

Nutrition Spoke

How has your nutritional intake been, on average, over the last twelve weeks? If you always eat fresh, balanced, nutritious, low fat meals, then place your mark near the upper end of the scale. But if you survive totally on beer, pizza and chocolate, then head down to the other end.

Emotional Spoke

If you are emotionally balanced, and how you quantify this will be open to conjecture, then you will more than likely cry occasionally,

laugh often, have some sad or flat days and some really happy days and will generally roll along with the roller-coaster of life. If this sort of emotional life seems familiar, then place your score toward the 100 end. If, on the other hand, you cry every day or laugh uncontrollably or fly off the handle at the slightest provocation, then you might want to consider something a bit lower.

Mental Spoke

Please don't confuse this with IQ or a 'smartness' rating. The mental spoke is about how active your grey matter is. It's not about the amount of intelligence you have, but how you use the intelligence you have. Do you find your work stimulating? Do you have any interesting hobbies? How much do you read or take an active interest in world news or discussions on politics? Remember that *you* are setting the standards here and just because you aren't interested in the political aspirations of the Left Wing in Bovinia, it doesn't mean you're boring. What we are talking about here is, by your standards, is your mind active or not?

Spiritual Spoke

By far the most difficult to define is the Spiritual spoke. We are not necessarily talking religion here, but if following a particular doctrine is important to your spiritual growth, then by all means mark your score on this line according to how much you actively involve yourself with this aspect of your life. Some people define their spirituality in terms of energy levels and how they feel connected to the planet and the universe. Others allot the term to anything that doesn't fit comfortably under any of the other headings. I have friends who tell me that tending their garden is, for them, a spiritual experience. Whatever your definition, only you will know if it is important to you and whether or not you are seeking to strengthen this area or let it look after itself.

Personally, I only discovered the importance of the spiritual side of me when I felt like I had all the other spokes handled, and yet I still wasn't happy. I have a clear memory of waking up one morning and saying, 'It's not here!' The meaning of life was not in achieving the results I was supposed to achieve and accumulating the material possessions that I had thought were going to make me happy. Mind you, they didn't make me unhappy either; it's just that I didn't yet have the full picture without the development of my spiritual spoke. For many it is more likely to be the hub of the wheel rather than a spoke, but that is another decision for you to ponder.

Learning from Your Wheel

When you have placed a mark on each spoke of the wheel, take your pen again and with a flowing, circular type of motion, go from spoke to spoke joining the marks you've made and draw what will probably be a rough, odd shaped circle. How does it look? What you have here is a pictorial representation of where you are with regard to your health and lifestyle. In a workshop situation we usually get many different shapes, but the common theme seems to be that almost everyone has a 'flat spot' somewhere. If this was a wheel on your vehicle through life, and I suggest that it is, then would your ride be smooth or bumpy? Which area or areas do you have to work on to take out the wobble?

Some people produce a wheel that is balanced, but the circle is very small. This result can be arrived .t by only applying minimal effort to all areas of your life – but I can't imagine it being much of a life. If you've ever wondered why your life seems to be out of control, maybe a glance at your Wheel of Health will give you some clues as to why that is happening. Good health is about much more than just bean shoots and press-ups. Effective stress management goes hand in hand with maintaining a healthy body and an active, well balanced lifestyle. There's a part of our sub-conscious that knows when we are out of control and even produces those little voices in our heads that tell us what we *should* be doing – but most of us either don't hear them or ignore the message. When we do act on the information and lose that five extra kilograms, start that degree we've always dreamed of getting or say no to the second helping of chocolate truffles, the feel good we get from doing something positive flows over into all areas of our lives. This in turn increases our ability to cope with the daily stresses of life. The Holistic Wheel of Health is a tool for developing awareness of the way we are living our lives. From these awarenesses we can construct a vision of our future, the way we would like it to be. To repeat something I said at the start of this section:

'When we feel good, we do good!'...and I know it's grammatically incorrect, but the rhyme is important!

And in <u>YOUR</u> life...

1. What were the biggest surprises when you drew your wheel? Why? Which broken expectations triggered those surprises?

2. Looking at the events associated with each spoke, which do you have control over? How can you exercise that control to modify the event next time?

3. How did you evaluate your scores on each spoke? Did you give yourself credit for the aspects of your wheel that work well? Or did you focus on berating yourself for achieving poor results?

4. What new creative expectations will you construct based on the awareness you have gained from your wheel? Go on! Set your SMARTER goals and paint a mental picture of your new, balanced lifestyle.

5. If you have created a Treasure Map following the suggestion at the end of Chapter 3, make sure you add some images from your Wheel e.g. A photograph of you out walking or in the gym; or perhaps a picture of your garden, where you feel a spiritual connection; or maybe a copy of the prospectus from a university you dream about attending.

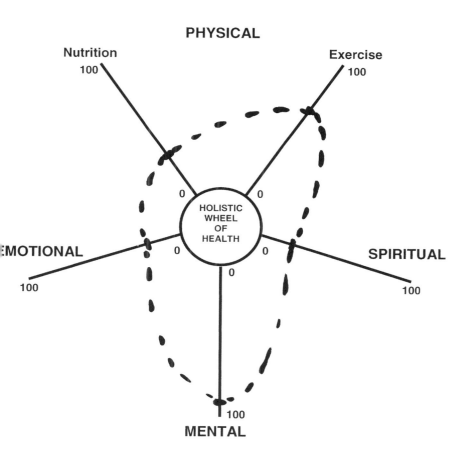

PHYSICAL

Nutrition
100

Exercise
100

0   0

HOLISTIC
WHEEL
OF
HEALTH

EMOTIONAL   0   0   SPIRITUAL

100   0   100

100
MENTAL

Figure 4
Here is how my wheel looked the first time I did this exercise.
I could instantly see where I needed to spend more energy.

LIFESTYLE MATTERS

IN THIRTY WORDS OR LESS...

'Balancing our lives can be as simple
as being aware of where we are
so that we can choose 'healthy'
Enlightened Responses
to get us where we want to go.'

CHAPTER ELEVEN

BELONGING

Once I have balanced my wheel of health, or have at least removed the major wobbles, where do I take my new found sense of self? Where do I fit in amidst the other six billion or so people on the planet? The longer I live, the more it becomes apparent to me that the answers to life's most puzzling questions lie in wait, just below the surface, obscured by their own simplicity. We have learned so much as a species – technically, medically, psychologically – but the 'big ones' almost always seem to elude us, like:

Who am I and where do I belong?

We spend most of our lives trying to find out where we fit in. Do you remember how you felt when you found you were part of the gang... and then again when you discovered you weren't? How many different 'gangs' have you joined, left or been excluded from since those first anxious expeditions into the schoolyard?

I joined the Always in Minor Trouble Gang by being consistently cheeky in school and was asked to spend considerable amounts of time standing outside the headmaster's office. Returning to the playground was accompanied (in my head at least) by a brass band belting out a triumphal march and choruses of 'What happened? How many cuts of the cane did you get?' Minor notoriety was infinitely superior to obscurity.

The Good at Sports Gang was always slightly out of reach because of my gross incompetence at cricket and rugby. Anyway, why would I want to carry the ball if I was going to be pursued by a marauding hoard of overweight, overdeveloped, adolescent gladiators, hell bent on driving me, ball and all, into the turf? When I finally found a sport to excel at – I became a champion teenage cyclist – I had to join another specialist gang called a Cycling Club where my particular talents were appreciated. Succeeding at just any sport certainly didn't grant me entry into the cricket and football hall of fame at school, but I must admit to noticing a certain amount of respect being afforded

me due to my prominence in a field *they* knew nothing about. They now just ignored me instead of ridiculing me.

As school days drew to their inevitable close my attention was focussed on that question which had been poked at me since I first learnt to talk. 'What are you going to do when you grow up?' My friends and family tell me constantly that this is an eventuality with which I needn't be concerned, but as my high school days came to an end it seemed the burning question was having the heat turned up.

One afternoon while walking to the station from school, the conversation turned to 'careers', which left me wondering if this was anything like 'getting a job'. A few of us 4D Woodwork and Metalwork boys, who weren't planning to go on to Senior High School, found ourselves in a gaggle of 4A History and Latin swats with distinctions and degrees in their sights. After a brief discussion between them of the relative merits of a Law, Medicine or a Science career, the snootiest of all turned to me and asked what my plans were. Stunned to be even considered worthy of questioning I blurted out that I was leaving school and taking up an apprenticeship in the printing industry.

'Why don't you stay on and get a degree in something', he sneered. Quick as a flash I replied with 'Um... er ... well.' Fully realising my dilemma, the second snootiest surprisingly jumped to my rescue, arguing that, 'Some people just aren't intelligent enough to go on to higher education!' Chuffed at having a hero from the bastions of academia stoop to my defence, I took a deep breath, puffed out my chest and bursting with the pride of asserting my position in the scholastic pecking order I chimed in with a most emphatic, 'Yeah!'

It wasn't until at least 10 years later that I started to realise that I'd been sold a pup. Up until I was almost 30, I had it firmly entrenched in my thinking that the Academic Qualifications Gang would never accept me as a member. I was wrong. And I'm not saying that this goal is possible or even desirable for everyone, but whatever our goals, aims, ambitions or dreams, it is always our thinking that will either help or hinder us. Awareness of our individual talents and abilities, strengths and weaknesses, will give us a launching pad for whatever course of action, education, job or career path we wish to pursue.

So, what *gang*, or should I say gangs, do I belong to now? As far as possible I aim to not let my thinking lock me into any set pattern or routine, so automatically I am inducted into the Rebel Gang, or the Getting Older But Trying Not To Conform Gang. And merely by being who I am, I find myself a fully bona fide member of many gangs. Being over forty-five years old, I am a somewhat reluctant member of the Middle Aged Gang. A recent wedding has put me in the Second Marriage Gang; my two children make me part of the Parent Gang and the appearance of a grandchild dragged me kicking and screaming (initially) into the Grandparent Gang. It is unavoidable! While I live (and even when I don't) I will find myself linked with others with whom I share an interest, qualification, personality type, automobile (Volkswagen Camper drivers all wave to each other!) or any one of an infinite number of criteria.

So... what's the lesson in all this?

It matters not which group or gang we belong to. The key to our individuality is the way we choose to think. By becoming aware of and observing our own thought processes we can learn to respond objectively, lovingly, rationally or inspirationally to any given event or situation. Do I mean we can *choose* our responses? YES! Even our primary urges for food, shelter, protection and sex still require a response. We can no longer blame these urges or desires for the results in our lives. It is, as it has always been, not a problem of *what happens*, but 'How do I respond to what happens?' While I am here, in this body, on this planet, things will happen to me. I can either use these things as tools to create what I want or as weapons to slay my enthusiasm and halt my progress.

'While I have a mind, I have a choice'

I choose to be a member of the Isn't This Interesting, How Can I Enjoy This And Use It To Help Me Move Forward Gang. This attitude automatically places me in with a group of people who view the world in a similar way to me. One method of defining the many different slants on life is through the term *Personality*. Which Personality Gang do I belong to? Which do you belong to? The next chapter may provide you with some clues.

And in <u>YOUR</u> life...

1. Your clothes, car, home, attitude, friends, behaviour; all give an indication of which groups or gangs you see yourself as part of. The following questions may help to raise your awareness.

Are you a { suit / flash car / bright colour / dine in / travelling / fast talking / married / parent / trade / tense } or a { casual clothes / practical car / pale colour / dine out / non-travelling / slow talking / single / non-parent / professional / relaxed } person

2. Look at your expectation of others. Are you critical or accepting of their different allegiances? Are they really stupid for supporting a certain football team or driving a particular model of car? If you do think these things, then are you saying that you will only be accepting of them if they support the same team or drive the same car as you? (or at least one that you like) Is that the kind of world you want; a world where everyone agrees with you?

BELONGING

IN THIRTY WORDS OR LESS...

'Awareness of the many different 'life views' will allow us to empathise with others and choose **Enlightened Responses** that will help to fill their and our need to belong.'

I belong to the People Who Get Silly Photographs
Taken With Their Hand On Mt Everest Gang.

CHAPTER TWELVE

PERSONALITY

Common Behaviours

One of the groups to which each of us belongs is of those with whom we share a similar range of habits and behaviours. I'm hoping we agree here that there are indeed many ways of looking at and relating to the world in which we live. Using habits as an indicator, we can discover many of these differences in the way we each handle every-day situations. The answers you give to the following questions will, like it or not, set you apart from millions of others who do it another way.

Consider each of the questions below for just a moment:

- How much toothpaste do you apply to your toothbrush? ¼ inch? ½ inch? Enough to cover all the bristles? On which side of your mouth do you start brushing? How do you remove the excess water from your brush after you have rinsed out the toothpaste? Are you a flicker?... a tapper?... do you dry it on your towel?... or do you just throw it back into its holder still dripping?

- Do you sit up straight or are you an habitual sloucher?

- When you get into your car, what do you do first; start the engine, turn on the radio or fasten your seatbelt?

The previous are all examples of physical habits, but what are the mental rituals you cling to? Like:

- Are you a worrier or an 'It'll all be OK' type?

- Do you get in first or stand back and wait?

- Are you volatile or placid?

- Are you a 'look after number one' person or a 'look after everyone else' person?

- Do you like or loathe these sorts of quizzes and psycho-babble?

Part of the game we are playing here has to do with the way we only

focus on certain parts of the environment. We all have an inbuilt system called a Reticular Activating System or RAS. It doesn't matter if we don't know how it works; the point is that we all have one and in fact wouldn't be able to survive without it. It's tucked away somewhere at the base of our brain and protects us from information overload. It heightens our awareness to certain aspects of our environment to which we have attached some importance and ignores data that is not relevant. It is an integral part of our perception filter. You've probably experienced it when you've just decided to buy a certain brand of car. For the two weeks before you actually collect it and drive away from the car lot, your RAS will constantly bombard you with anything that even remotely reminds you of this impending purchase. It practically yells at you... 'There's one... and there's another one!' Can you imagine what it would be like if you gave that much attention to every car on the road. We have to have this filter or we'd go crazy. It will also do things like; focus on anything that is small and shiny when you are looking for your keys, or, when you are sleeping, it will screen out all noise except the sound of your child crying.

I was listening recently to a lecture by Dr David Suzuki, the world famous environmental campaigner, and he admitted to not having, and more importantly, not wanting, an internet connection. He said that the Net was an incredible source of information, but WE DON'T NEED MORE INFORMATION! He called it an 'info-glut'. The message that came through to me was that I need to take more time to act on the information I already have.

Our RAS is set mainly by experience and is a major part of our personality. It assists us by only letting through those pieces of information that will match our assessment of what has been:

        (a) successful or comfortable in the past, or
        (b) what has caused us pain or anguish

It points out what it thinks will be good for us and what it thinks will not. So how can we get it to work more effectively for us?

When I was first married with a young child, I took on a night cleaning job to supplement my meagre apprentice's income. I had only been doing it for about three weeks but I was amazed how quickly I had settled into the pattern. I would finish my day job at four o'clock, grab a bite to eat and then from four-thirty until nine-thirty at night I supervised the cleaning of a Department of Main Roads building near Sydney's Central railway station. Weekends were hardly occasions for big spending and sometimes for entertainment on a Saturday night we would go down to the airport, watch the planes take off and the people coming and going, and dream about the day when it would be us heading off overseas. On one of these nights, wandering around the arrival halls, baby cradled in my arms, I started stooping down and picking up pieces of lint and fluff off the carpet on the stairs! 'What are you doing?' my wife said.

It was quite simple really. In three short weeks my RAS had been fine-tuned to notice problems that could hinder my survival and consequently the well-being of my family. If I didn't notice the lint > I wouldn't be doing my job efficiently > I might lose my job > we wouldn't be able to cope financially > I wouldn't be fulfilling my obligation to provide food and shelter to the family unit. Unfortunately it was so strong an impulse it overpowered that part of my brain that knew it was my day off! Is this an over dramatisation of a trivial event? Perhaps. But to me it illustrated how quickly I can fall into a pattern of behaviour and how little I was aware of it happening. If my focus on my environment was reset in just a few short weeks, then maybe I can choose to change what I focus on in the world, or at least the aspects I focus on e.g. positive or negative, happy or sad.

And maybe even *changing* is an ineffective and difficult way of creating the results I want. Maybe I need to overlay some new patterns instead of changing the old ones. I don't know about you, but I haven't had a lot of success at changing things about me when I've tackled them head on. It's a bit like mating elephants – lots of effort, lots of noise and its ages before you get a result!

Maybe Awareness can lead to CHANGE

Habits, by definition, are behaviours, practised often without our awareness. We don't always know we're doing them. A set of particular habits or behaviours constitutes a *personality*. As you already know, it is usually quite easy to see the basic flaws in another person's personality by observing their inappropriate behaviours i.e. the way they interact with their environment and the people with whom they

come in contact. (In other words, those stupid things they do and say which we don't agree with and of course don't do ourselves because we are *enlightened beings*) As you will also probably know, this 'other person' isn't always aware of their own particular behaviours and will often deny their existence. It then logically follows that the same is also probably true for us.

We are often unaware of many of the particular traits and behaviours that go to make up our own personalities.

Practising self observation exercises will eventually expose many of our previously hidden techniques for dealing with the world. Honestly appraising each situation and in particular, our thoughts about that situation, and then becoming aware of the resultant behaviours, will be of enormous benefit. We can't modify it if we don't know we're doing it. And we won't know we're doing it if we don't stop and look for it. Objectively observing our own and others' behaviour will enable us to choose more **Enlightened Responses.** Being aware of our personality traits can have a major impact on the way we see our life experiences, including the way we go about setting our personal goals.

Doesn't everyone think like me?

Once I have started identifying my own interactions with the world around me, can I assume that everyone else will have similar sets of behaviours (personalities)? Not likely. Your own experience will tell you that not everyone sees the world the way you do and you will have developed your own system for categorising other people based on some of their identifiable behavioural characteristics. Your system will probably have a category for Shy People. There may be another called Aggressive, possibly with a sub-set named Violent People. There'll probably be Jokers, Workaholics, Emotional/Artistic types and even Pain In The Butt Avoid At All Cost types. Come on, admit it! We all do it, don't we?

Personality Assessment Systems

So... are formalised systems for assessing and categorising personalities useful? (Be aware that to a large extent your personality will govern your answer to that question.) Will the information gained from studying these systems be of benefit to me and how much of this information will I have to acquire before it improves my understanding and makes my life easier? (Which is what we're all after isn't it?)

Answer: Even the most basic acknowledgement that not everyone views the world the way I do, can lead me to the more profound acceptance of the idea that:

'My way is not the only way to look at life and that perhaps there is no ultimate right way, just many different ways'.

Gestalt Psychologists:
'argued that human beings have certain innate principles of thinking and that they tend to look at problems in certain ways, which, unless the individual is careful, can lead to rigid ways of tackling things'
FROM 'PSYCHOLOGY – AN INTRODUCTION.'

On a sliding scale, where 0 indicates no knowledge and 100 indicates complete knowledge, at what point will someone else's previously collected observations become helpful? Should I do a university degree on the subject or will even a little learning be helpful? How much information will make a difference? A simple analogy may help give clarity.

Fire has been used by human beings for thousands of years for everything from roasting lizards and heating caves through to setting it under a twenty-story rocket ship to propel it to mars. The accumulated research about this basic element could fill a library. Yet even the most basic knowledge that it feels hot, will stop me from sticking my hand in it. It could also prevent me from freezing to death, and that's got to be a useful!

The knowledge that my wife is a perfectionist and is driven by a desire to do the *right* thing and be the *right* sort of person, formed a basis for our relationship to grow instead of terminate. What helped her to accept me as I am, was an understanding that my genetic make-up and childhood experiences created a need in me to always have many options to choose from and to always want to see what's on the other side of the hill. With each of us armed with this knowledge, we could create a mostly harmonious relationship between the often incompatible Perfectionist and Optionist.

One personality assessment system (and there are many) that I have found extremely enlightening is the Enneagram. Originally devised by Muslim mystics and holy men known as Sufis, about one thousand years ago, this system has recently been shown to hold up well under modern psychological scrutiny.

Do I need to know everything there is to know about the Enneagram before it will be of use to me?

Well, I find the more I learn, the easier it is for me to understand my own behaviour and the particular idiosyncrasies of those around me. But the greatest benefit to me was gained the day I was introduced to the Enneagram. Where in the past I had often seen the beliefs of others to be antagonistic to my own, suddenly I had a glimpse of the bigger picture. I now saw my own views as a small but important piece of the puzzle; not the whole puzzle. Separating the deed from the do-er, I began to see people as they are. I saw that we all still have the same pure heart and combination of curiosity and wonder with which we were born, and overlaid on that genetic cocktail we have fashioned a personality from our experiences of the world and our own cultural environment. To protect us and make us feel safe and comfortable, we have adopted a set of tools, called habits. Some of these habits were learnt at a very young age and may still be serving us well, and yet others were probably state of the art when we were toddlers, launching ourselves at life's learning curve, but they have limited positive effect in the boardroom. The 'tantrum' is a prime example of one of these outmoded behaviours.

> 'The wonderful advantage of cultural information over genetic is that it is so much easier to change and update. The limitations of cultural information are that it has to be imposed on the genetic background of a hunter/gatherer ape, and we pick it up as we go along until it becomes part of our mental furniture.'
> FROM 'EVER SINCE ADAM AND EVE'
> BY MALCOLM POTTS AND ROGER SHORT

Continuing on with that mental image, the bigger the piece of mental furniture, the more difficult it is to remove. Some habits are like scatter rugs and we can flick them out once they start to look tatty or have outlived their usefulness. Some are like iron-framed pianos with no wheels. We need help to even nudge them closer to the door.

Once I accepted that every individual has developed a unique set of habits; once I saw that there certainly are many other ways of seeing and dealing with the same situation; and once I stepped away from my little ivory tower of self righteousness – I felt a wave of calm descend on me. I realised that I don't have to go through life rigidly defending my own beliefs from perceived attacks. I also discovered that it is unreasonable for me to expect that others should think the way I do. In my mind, and particularly in my personal Thought Evaluation System, they now have ceased to be wrong – they're just different. I may agree or disagree; I may see their actions as appropriate or inappropriate; their methods may be effective or ineffective, but as far as possible I aim to view their ideas or behaviours as neither good nor bad. They are just the way they are. I can still live a fruitful and fulfilling life, produce results when I need to, defend my beliefs, my loved ones and my assets, but without the added burden of the self-righteousness that comes with judging someone else's thoughts or actions as wrong.

So... can the Enlightened Response technique help to create harmonious relationships with others?

For me – obviously from my biased point of view – the answer is 'yes'. Observing and understanding my own thoughts and behaviours can lead me to accept, if not understand, the behaviour of others, which in turn adjusts my expectations and eliminates judgement, which is the source of much of my anxiety. I can also learn from the other types around me. There will be many situations in my life that will be easier to manage if I can adopt one or more of their more appropriate behaviours to tackle the task in hand.

For those of you who need or would like more information on using the Enneagram as a tool for creating awareness, following is a brief overview of this amazingly accurate and detailed system of personality assessment.

The Enneagram

As babies we all start with a similar view of our environment, but we quickly learn that some things work for us and some things don't. We

mentally store away the experiences that were successful in gaining us what we wanted and in the future decide to watch for favourable conditions to reappear so that we can use the same technique again. Conversely, the negative experiences are stored as well and we often choose not to go down that road again for fear of reproducing a failure.

The Enneagram suggests that there are three main groups of people in the world that have basically different 'focuses of attention'.

The three groups are:

Instinctual, Emotional and Mental

The Instinctual types are those practical, no nonsense, 'take me as I am', down to earth types whose main focus is on control – of themselves and others. Anger is the power behind their energy, but it isn't always obvious.

As the title suggests, the Emotional types are focussed on and motivated by their own feelings and the feelings of others.

Mental types are the great thinkers of the world. Everything in their lives is both preceded and followed by much careful, and often not so careful thought. They are careful because they are fearful, even though they might not look it.

These three groups are then each subdivided into another three, according to whether their focus is:

- Introverted
- Suppressed or denied
- Extroverted

The Instinctual Types

Perfectionists: Introverted instinctual types turn their anger inward and become focussed on getting it right. Quality and correctness are paramount.
Mediators: The middle of the three instinctual types suppress and deny their anger and try to keep everyone happy. They dislike conflict.
Controllers: The extroverted instinctual types use their anger, either overtly or covertly, to control their environment. Others see them as powerful.

The Emotional Types

Artists / Tragic-romantics: Introverted emotional types focus on how things make them feel. They see themselves as unique and different.

Achievers: The middle emotional types suppress their feelings until the work is done. And it's never done. Success and their own image are important.

Supporters: Extroverted emotional types understand and feel other people's feelings. They are the eternal social workers of the world.

The Mental Types

Researchers: These introverted mental types are happier in the back room, working it out, than out front talking about it. Fear of exposure keeps him/her hidden.

Questioners: Suspicious, sceptical and wary, the suppressed fear of these mental types will cause them to be staunch allies if you have them on side.

Optionists: The extroverted mental type are forever thinking about and planning new, fun and exciting things to do, and so avoid having to face their fears.

Famous Enneagram Types

Here are some famous Enneagram types to give you a feel for the way they appear to others.

Emotional

Supporter	Princess Diana, Mother Teresa, Alan Alda,
Achiever	Tom Cruise, Carl Lewis, Bill Clinton
Tragic/Romantic	Meryl Streep, Ally McBeal, Marlon Brando

Mental

Researcher	Anthony Hopkins, Howard Hughes, Buddha
Questioner	Woody Allen, Mel Gibson, Marilyn Monroe
Optionist	Robin Williams, Barbara Streisand, Tim Allen

Instinctual

Perfectionist	Harrison Ford, Anne Robinson, Hilary Clinton
Mediator	John Candy, Barney Rubble, The Dalai Lama
Controller	John Wayne, Clint Eastwood, Fred Flintstone

Learning from other types

There is so much we can learn from other personality types and we can use this knowledge to experiment with handling situations using their strategies, especially when our own seem to be failing or inadequate. A problem I may approach with fear and trepidation may turn out to be a situation in which another type may thrive. Conversely, my idea of a fun night out could possibly cause cold sweats in a less outgoing personality. Here's an example:

For a tough, no nonsense, practical, Controller type foreman of a maintenance crew working on the Sydney Harbour Bridge, a half dozen loose rivets (out of a total of 6 million) would be an irritation. A bridge this size and this age, well, he'd say, 'It's to be expected'

One hundred loose rivets – 'Now, we'll have to replace them, so that's an expense, and we'll have to take a couple of people off the painting crew to do the work. We'd better bring in the engineer to check it out...' Suddenly it's becoming a problem!

Then he turns up to work one morning and five hundred rivets have sheared off causing a girder to snap and the road to give way. A truck has overturned...Disaster!

But each individual would respond in a slightly different way. An anxious, worrying, sceptical Questioner foreman would probably have his mind on the disaster from the spotting of the first loose rivet. The Optionist would be working out what he would still have time to do after work that night. And the Supporter would be concerned about how many people it would inconvenience. The important point to realise is that the adrenalin hit from these situations is directly proportionate to the way we view it; and the way we view it is intricately linked with our personality or our behavioural style.

One evening, a friend at a dinner party asked me to give an abbreviated overview of the Enneagram. On the table in front of me sat a pale green paper napkin folded into a fancy fan shape. Picking it up and examining it I said:

- The Perfectionist would look at this and say, 'It's not folded very neatly'.

- The Supporter would ask if any one else needed it.

- The Achiever would imagine how much they could sell it for and begin looking for a sales team and customers.

- The Tragic/Romantic would say that the colour reminded them of a shirt an old lover of theirs used to wear.

- The Researcher would say nothing, but begin to work out what it was made from and how he could get a machine to fold it, and then he would mentally calculate how much profit could be made from selling it.

- The Questioner would worry if they had the right one. 'Is it mine? Should I give it to someone else, and if so, why?'

- The Optionist would put it on their head and wear it as a party hat and then say 'Look at me!'

- The Controller would wipe their mouth with it and comment that it was 'only a stupid napkin.'

- And the Mediator would give it to anyone, as long as it kept the peace.

Note: We are never totally locked into a single set of behaviours. We are naturally a blend of several types, but we will tend to have a set of strategies for dealing with life and will often automatically default to them, especially when under pressure.

For serious students of the Enneagram there are many publications available on the subject from various authors, but I especially recommend anything by Helen Palmer, from whom I borrowed most of the names of the different types.

Overview of how our personalities are created

It is almost universally accepted that our personalities and our behaviours – the way we 'do life' – begin with our inherited material and are then shaped by the environment of our formative years. i.e. what we get from nature and how we are nurtured. Scientists have discovered that the hard wiring of our brains is more or less complete by the time we are seven or eight years old.

...'we find that the most important thing is the interaction between what we have inherited and our experience as we grow up.'
FROM 'PSYCHOLOGY – AN INTRODUCTION.'

The question is: Do we have any control over either of these developmental components? I don't remember having much control over my environment as I was growing up, and I certainly didn't have any control over the gene pool from which I slithered. Just take a look around you at all the people you know and all the people you meet every day and try to see their personalities and their behaviours as separate from them as beings. Our personalities are merely tools that have been shaped to help us cope with life. If your gene pool was different to mine (and it was) and your childhood experiences of life were different to mine (and they were) then your personality, beliefs and values will be different to mine (and they are!)

Briefly: The personalities you love and the personalities you clash with, were developed during a period when the owner had no control. On top of that, the owner of the personality usually has no idea of exactly what they do or the way in which they do it. How easy it is to see someone else's strengths and weaknesses and be virtually blind to our own.

'But as adults we have choice' I hear you say.

Yes, and on what foundations do we make those choices? The choices we make as adults can only come from a selection of choices to which we were exposed as children. A teenage Nepalese Sherpa girl would never even consider travelling to the next village by bus, as she has never seen a bus. A child raised in an environment of constant conflict will probably adopt one of the behaviour patterns he or she most often observed; aggression or submission. Or perhaps they will develop any one of a variety of coping mechanisms, like... manipulation, or entertaining the warring parties, or becoming invisible – 'If they can't see me, they can't hurt me.'

'But what about the child raised in a loving environment who still ends up becoming violent or anti-social?

The question here is still the same. What innate tendencies did this child inherit and how did that shape his perceptions of his environment? I'm almost certain that babies don't choose to become belligerent teenagers, manipulative mothers or controlling fathers, but if they do, then what precipitates those choices?

> '*It is pointless to be angry with other people, because their delusions (false impressions or distorted views of reality) are what drive them to act the way they do. In a way it's a kind of insanity – and if someone was insane you would not judge them harshly as you would know it was something over which they had no control.*'
>
> FROM THE TEACHINGS OF THE DALAI LAMA,
> DHARAMSALA, INDIA, MARCH 1998.

Through self observation we can heighten our awareness of our often concealed beliefs and behaviour patterns, enabling us to manage those parts of our personalities that hold us back.

OBSERVE your own behaviour patterns

ACCEPT that some changes may need to be made

CHOOSE the most appropriate response

And in <u>YOUR</u> life...

1. Study the way you do things. When practising the self observations in Chapter 8, add an extra dimension by considering exactly how you perform a certain task compared to how someone else might do it. Do these behaviours cause you to categorise yourself a certain way?

2. Once you have put yourself in a particular behavioural style group, look at the way you categorise others. Ask yourself what behaviours you are comfortable with and which ones you are not and why?

3. Identify the behaviours that cause you to be in conflict or out of harmony with other people. What do you do that annoys or irritates them? Do you have the courage to ask them? How are you going to change if you don't know what you need to change?

4. What can you choose to do differently? Do other people have some effective behaviours you would like to copy?

5. Stop for a moment right now and tune your RAS to notice anything in your field of view that is coloured *red*. Observe how everything else in your field of view becomes less significant – almost ceases to exist while you have a *red* focus. It is the same with points of view. It is virtually impossible to see someone else's if your RAS is firmly locked on your own.

PERSONALITY

IN THIRTY WORDS OR LESS...

'Through self observation we can heighten awareness of our often concealed beliefs and behaviour patterns, and choose **Enlightened Responses** to manage those partsof our personalities that hold us back.'

CHAPTER THIRTEEN

CREATING PEACE IN MY RELATIONSHIPS

What can I expect from my relationships?

And here I'm not just referring to intimate relationships, which we'll discuss shortly. Our relationships we have with other people are mostly in our own heads. It follows then that we have relationships with every single person we've ever met, seen, heard, read about, heard about, seen pictures of, watched on television or seen in the movies. Much of these relationships is based on what we hear them say, the way they look, the way they treat others and a huge amount can be attributed to transference - of whom or what do they remind us?

I've spent a great deal of time over the last few years studying personality types, and in particular, discovering which personalities produce different reactions in me and why? There's a certain personality type, and set of accompanying behaviours, which reminds me of my brother. Consequently, any behaviour similar to his, especially when it's directed at me, will bring about the same feelings in me at the age of forty-nine as it did when I was just fourteen. This can be when I am merely observing the behaviour and not even directly involved. The relationship I have with, or feelings I get from observing, this person whom I may not even know, are transferred from a previous relationship and projected or overlaid onto this new person.

I have run workshops where a person has stood up about half an hour into my presentation and screamed abuse at me, yelling 'I hate people like you who...' Notice, it's not usually 'I hate you', but a virtual admission that it is 'people like you', which generally translates to: 'There's a whole group of people, including you, that remind me of some person or incident (whether consciously remembered or not) sometime in my past. You are here, and the original perpetrators aren't, so I'll take out my anger on you!'

Of course it has been of great benefit to me to learn the basics of this everyday occurrence and disassociate myself from the emotion it brings up, for them and for me. That doesn't mean to say that I can walk away from my personal responsibilities. There will be times when my behaviour will upset someone, but even their judgement and my judgment is based on a set of beliefs laid down much earlier in both our lives. The basic standpoint from which we expect and judge as adults, was very firmly established by the time we were teenagers, and for most of us by the time we were seven or eight years old. This is about the time when the hard wiring of the brain is completed leaving us with behaviour patterns that we will repeat over and over again as adults. It was both a scary and comforting thing for me to learn that, by and large, the way I view the world, and the people in it, is based on a value system that was fundamentally complete by the time I was about ten years old.

'The adult in me may know many things about the world, but I often wonder if the seven year old enjoyed it more, before he refined his ability to create expectations and make judgements.'

We've all had the challenge of trying to change what's in someone else's head, and in my experience it meets with limited success. As Ashleigh Brilliant once wrote:

'Why do I keep coming home every time I try to trace my troubles to their source?'

My relationship with you, is in me, not in you.

Expecting the Perfect Partner

In some cultures it is expected that when a young man or woman reaches the marrying age, they will seek out, or often be introduced to, someone whose credentials place them roughly within the 'possible partner' ballpark. It is expected by their family that they will form a permanent union and make something out of what they have. Combining their raw materials they form something akin to a chunk of clay from which they are expected to build a relationship. It's a bit like two novice potters making their first pot. If this relationship pot is to survive, it will have to be moulded and shaped, baked and glazed, until it becomes hardened with the experience of time, impervious to the ravages of co-existence, protected by the skills of cooperation and mindful of the dangers of co-dependence. Saying 'No!' is not usually an option, so they just get on with it. I'm not suggesting that we all should adhere to this system of spouse selection, but there's possibly something to be learned from the way they are required to work at it and not bail out at the first sign of rough weather.

We want to find the finished pot!

We are not content with the age-old process of research and development. With our modern, western approach to mating, we want to walk into the relationships department store and choose one off the rack, hoping that the experiences that this 'off the shelf' lover has encountered has led them to exactly the same point on the emotional growth trail as ours have. Fat chance!

When we find someone who makes our pulse quicken, a rush of adrenalin to the heart (and groin) sends us into a romantic tail-spin. The voice in the head is yelling:
'This is the one! I've found her for you. The missing jig-saw piece, the needle in the haystack, your soul mate, the only person in the whole world who has had a set of experiences which have prepared them for their only possible destiny – to be your one and only True Love!'

No, ...I don't think so. But could this societally induced expectation set us up for a life of anxiety? Will we either worry because we haven't yet found our Mr or Ms Wonderful, low mileage, low maintenance, 'my life will be perfect from now on' life partner, or, when we've eventually found him/her, will we spend our time sitting around waiting for the pot to crack?

How many of us have fallen – a more accurate description of the process than it would first seem – in love, only to find the gloss finish starting to craze or the handle chipping, when the road to Blissville develops a few potholes? Mentally we scurry back to the store shouting, 'I was robbed! I want a new one!' or 'at least send the old one back to the potter (counsellor) to be fixed'. And if the pot doesn't want to be fixed to match our idea of perfection, or more often than not, can't be changed to meet our demands, then we scrap the whole pot and start again i.e. start the search for a new, finished pot, not a search for more clay.

Observing the successful (purely from my point of view) relationships I have encountered over the years, has led me to believe even more solidly the premise by which I am attempting to live my life and on which this book is largely based.

> **'If I have no expectations then I have no need to be**
> **disappointed when they are not met.'**

Very simply, I try to have an expectation that all eventualities are possible, so that nothing ever surprises me. If I hold the expectation that it 'will' happen, and drop the expectation that it 'should' happen within my expected time frame, I can set myself up for a much easier ride.

Building a relationship from raw materials could mean that first of all I need to make sure that my own raw materials are the highest quality I can procure. Being aware of my own strengths, weaknesses, abilities and shortcomings is the basis for my acceptance of, and empathy for, others; and particularly my chosen partner. Through the filter of my own personality and belief system it is impossible for me to experience life from any point of view other than my own. Most scientists would agree that my perceptions are entirely based on two sets of circumstances:

1. My genetic make up – traits and behaviours inherited from my parents

2. My experiences of my life since conception (Yes, your memories started then too!)

...and no two sets of either of these are identical.

I recall meeting twelve-month-old identical twin girls whose experience of their family had already been altered by the responses they were getting. The day we met I commented to one of the parents that one of them seemed a little unhappy. 'Oh yes' came the reply, 'she's the serious one'. And whether she was or wasn't is irrelevant. The fact that they had already been labelled caused people to treat them differently, therefore bringing about a different life experience. If those around me tell everyone I meet that I'm 'the serious one', I will be treated with caution and the faces I encounter will be subtly different to the faces encountered by my gorgeous, 'Isn't she a happy little thing', sister.

My raw materials are my core beliefs about myself, my place in the world and my acceptance of, and interaction with, those with whom I share this planet. Perhaps I can adjust to an expectation of finding a partner with whom I share some basic, common ground and embrace and fall in love with the raw materials. More importantly, perhaps I need to learn to love the potting process, working toward perfection but resisting the urge to expect that it has to happen immediately. As human beings we are meant to make mistakes as part of the process of learning. It follows then that I am only perfect if I make mistakes.

Question: So, how do I learn to adjust my expectations?
Answer: By using self observation to develop awareness.

The 4-2-1 View of Relationships

On a practical level, I believe there are only FOUR things to be aware of in any of my relationships.

1. My own behaviour – my personality, habits etc
2. My partner's behaviour – their personality, habits etc
3. My partner's reactions and responses to my behaviour
4. My responses to my partner's behaviour

A further simplification is that I really have only TWO things to concern myself with. i.e. The only ones over which I have any control.

1. My behaviour
2. My responses to my partner's behaviour.

Which when looked at objectively, can be boiled down to only ONE aspect:

My Behaviour – as my responses are really just part of my own behaviour.

And what controls my behaviour? My thinking! See how I keep travelling in circles like the man with one foot nailed to the floor? I can no longer, in all honesty, go on blaming any other man, woman or event for my reactions. Only one person in my life has any power over my thinking and therefore my behaviour. It is only with awareness that I can start to recognise these well-ingrained habits and choose to have *enlightened responses to*, rather than *un-enlightened reactions against*, the people and events of my life.

And in <u>YOUR</u> life...

1. What expectations do you have about others with whom you have relationships? Are these expectations realistic?

2. In what way do the individual events of these relationships mis-match with your expectations?

3. Turning conflict into harmony requires that the expectation or the event or the evaluation needs to change. Look at the issues that cause upheaval in your relationships and decide which of the three is the most appropriate to change.

For example, the age-old argument about the washing up. I could change my expectation that my partner should do half of it, and instead, ask them to trade their half for something they would enjoy doing and I wouldn't.

Or...I could change the event by using paper plates and always dining out. (A friend tried this on her husband who subsequently decided that the event of doing the dishes was more appealing than the consequences of a huge credit card bill)

Or... I could change my evaluation of the event by assessing that the chores my partner performs instead of washing up are far more valuable than having clean crockery.

In other words, think about how your Enlightened Responses can create a win-win.

CREATING PEACE IN MY RELATIONSHIPS
IN THIRTY WORDS OR LESS...

'My relationships exist in my mind.
Observing my own thoughts and behaviours
will assist me to understand myself
and others and to choose more
Enlightened Responses.'

'I am convinced that neither of us wake up in the morning with a plan for how we can ruin the other person's day.'

CHAPTER FOURTEEN

WHAT IS AN ENLIGHTENED RESPONSE?

I hope that, having reached this point in the book, you have acquired sufficient information to answer the above question. If you are anything like me you might have skipped straight to this section out of curiosity, but regardless of whether you have arrived here via the long or the short route, the following may be of use.

Reactions, Responses and Enlightened Responses

At any point along the path of our lives we can employ more Enlightened Responses. To illustrate some examples of the various choices we have at any given moment, I have outlined some life events and have then divided the possibilities into Reactions, Responses and Enlightened Responses. But before proceeding it is worthwhile to consider the expectations that often precipitate these reactions and responses.

First of all, regarding my relationship with others, what are the expectations of both parties?

Mine: That I will go along on my daily path and do things that I believe will produce results that keep me feeling satisfied and content, if not always happy.

Theirs: That they will go along on their daily life path and do things that they believe will produce results that keep them feeling satisfied and content, if not always happy.

Common ground? We almost certainly desire very similar results in our lives – peace, happiness, abundance – but just as certainly we use different methods for attaining them. While in pursuit of these goals our methods will often clash, but I am convinced that neither of us

153

woke in the morning with a plan for how we could ruin the other person's day.

General Expectations

*When I have an adverse **Reaction** to an event, my expectation was probably something like:*

I 'should' be able to go about my daily business without affecting other people and that other people will perceive things exactly the same way as I do.

*When I have a controlled (and sometimes judgemental) **Response** to an event, my expectation was probably something like:*

Other people will not always see things the way I do. They are wrong, but I am wise and I can see the error of their ways and will leave them to suffer along their life's journey and hope that they stay out of my way.

*When I have an **Enlightened Response** to an event, my expectation was probably something like:*

Others will never see the world exactly the way I do. Their inherited traits and mental processing of their life experiences has led them to a point where they believe their behaviour is the most appropriate for the given circumstances. I will not judge this behaviour as either good or bad, but will respond to it in a manner that serves and protects us both. I will always attempt to choose thoughts and behaviours that assist myself and others to harmoniously cohabit this planet.

Possible Choices

The Scene: I am driving along the highway and decide to slow down to turn into a roadside café. The driver of the car behind me, convinced that this has caused a major disruption to his journey, leans heavily on his horn, curses me extravagantly with a string of four letter Anglo-Saxon expletives and winds down his window so as to enable the offering of a visual message involving the waving of an arm and an animated, one fingered greeting.

Possible Reaction:

I throw my vehicle into a sideways shower of dust and gravel, braking suddenly enough to throw my passengers screaming in terror against their seatbelts, while I simultaneously swivel excitedly in my seat to return a reciprocal gesture from my personal repertoire.

My expectations that preceded this reaction were:

Other drivers will always be courteous and shouldn't react aggressively to my driving. I should reciprocate with matching aggression if they break my expectation.

Possible Response:

I choose to dismiss the event as not important enough to warrant the raising of my blood pressure and merely ignore the vociferous and gesticulated taunts of this obviously deranged driver from hell.

My expectations that preceded this response were:

Other drivers are not always courteous. I will dismiss them as poor, ignorant fools and understand that they are not as intelligent or wise as me.

Possible Enlightened Response:

I empathise with Mr or Mrs Road Rage and ponder on the possible catalogue of calamitous events in his or her life that have brought them to a point where they felt it necessary to unleash fifteen gallons of vitriol on an unsuspecting fellow traveller over a somewhat trivial misdemeanour. I calmly choose a course of action that I sincerely believe to be in the best interests of all concerned.

My expectations that preceded this Enlightened Response were:

Other drivers have problems and behavioural patterns of which I am not aware. Because of these, they will sometimes react aggressively as a reaction to something I do. It is possible that they see my behaviours as a threat to their safety or well-being. I will consider all this before I choose a response that I intend to benefit us both.

Other Examples in Brief

Raining

Reaction: 'Damn rain is spoiling my day!'
Response: 'I'll avoid going out, because of the rain.'

Enlightened Response: 'Fantastic! The rain gives me an opportunity to... and besides that, it'll help the grass grow.'

Stuck in traffic

Reaction: Tension, swearing and punching of the steering wheel.

Response: Listen to the radio.

Enlightened Response: Remember to leave home earlier next time or go via a different route. Relax my grip on the wheel and ponder on the good fortune that I am merely experiencing a result of the traffic snarl and that I am not the cause of it.

Very little food in the fridge

Reaction: Complain that there is nothing I like to eat.

Response: Order a talk-away meal.

Enlightened Response: Make a list of all the things I want to buy when next I shop, experiment with making a meal from the ingredients I do have and appreciate the fact that, unlike three quarters of the world, my next meal will probably be substantial and will happen in the not too distant future.

After 2 or 3 drinks

Reaction – 'I feel great. Let's get drunk'.

Response – 'I've had a few, so maybe just a couple more.'

Enlightened Response: 'I'm aware that I've had too much already. If I have any more I'll be too drunk to drive safely. If I do drive I could have an accident and hurt myself or someone else and if I get caught I could lose my license. On top of all that, I am punishing my liver and I'll feel terrible tomorrow. Bearing all that in mind, I'll stop drinking now.'

Waiting for someone

Reaction: 'I hate this. People are always letting me down. Waiting is boring.'

Response: 'I'll plan how I' am going to lecture this person when they arrive.'

Enlightened Response: 'Having expected that this might happen I have brought along a book to read and have already arranged that I will wait only a certain amount of time and then leave for my next appointment.'

Can't sleep

Reaction: Toss, turn, thump my pillow and wake my wife to tell her that I can't sleep.

Response: Get out of bed and work for hours until I get tired.

Enlightened Response: Briefly write down all the issues that are circulating in my head. Return to bed and practice self observation and/or visualise a peaceful, relaxing scene, constantly coaxing my mind back to the place that I want it. Expect that I will go to sleep shortly and in the mean time I will calm my thinking and therefore rest my mind.

Nothing on TV I want to watch

Reaction: Curse the networks and frantically channel-surf.

Response: Watch something I'm really not interested in just for the sake of filling in time.

Enlightened Response: Turn the TV off and do something that will give me a lift when completed. Read a book. Cook a meal. Write a letter.

No clean clothes to wear

Reaction: Don't go out.

Response: Go out wearing something old or dirty and feel self-conscious all evening.

Enlightened Response: Consider whether it is more important to go out and enjoy the evening or miss out because of a small housekeeping oversight. I could wash something quickly and dry it over the radiator; or wear something that is not my favourite but will serve the purpose. If I believe that my friends will judge me because of the condition of my clothes, then I might consider finding some new friends!

Someone speaks to me harshly

Reaction: Speak harshly in return.

Response: Devise a sarcastic and cutting response.

Enlightened Response: Consider that their anger is probably not directed at me but I am merely the object of their aggression in the present moment. Acknowledge their anger, recognise their right to have it, but make it clear that it is inappropriate to dump it on me. I will be more responsive to their requests if they approach me in a pleasant manner.

Food not good in restaurant

Reaction: Abuse the waiter and restaurant manager.

Response: Send the meal back making a show of my disapproval for the entertainment of the other diners.

Enlightened Response: Calmly speak to the waiter stating the specific reasons for my displeasure and offer some solutions – a discount or a new meal?

Wine not chilled

Reaction: Complain loudly or say nothing and resolve never to return.

Response: Drink the wine and suffer in silence.

Enlightened Response: Explain the problem to the waiter. Ask if there is perhaps another bottle of similar wine that is already chilled.

Children misbehaving

Reaction: Yell and dole out physical punishment.

Response: Control my anger and devise clever put-downs designed to belittle them and undermine their confidence, which I see as brashness.

Enlightened Response: Recognise that there is an obvious need here that is not being met and talk calmly to the child, clarifying the ground rules and the sort of behaviour expected of them.

Children behaving:

Reaction: Ignore them using the 'Let sleeping dogs lie' principle.

Response: Offer sugary and patronising praise that lets the child know that they have succeeded because they have pleased you.

Enlightened Response: Offer support and encouragement for their behaviour that allows them to appreciate exactly why it is beneficial to them and you.

Partner untidy:

Reaction: Nag and complain.

Response: Keep tidying up after them and don't say anything.

Enlightened Response: Agree on a set of ground rules. Explain to them that it is ineffective for me to operate outside those ground rules. Have an agreement that, if there are items left around in an untidy fashion, that I will bundle them up and place them in a receptacle for them to deal with at a later date. This way it moves from being my problem to being their problem. Keep renegotiating the ground rules.

And in <u>YOUR</u> life...

1. Recognise that there is **always** a choice and that:

    A reaction is human
    A response is effective
    An **Enlightened Response** is powerful and creative

2. Every reaction or response you have is probably (most likely, but not yet scientifically proven) preceded by a thought. Attempt to trace these reactions and responses back to their triggering thoughts. You can now choose to change the ones you don't like and repeat the ones you do.

WHAT IS AN ENLIGHTENED RESPONSE?

IN THIRTY WORDS OR LESS...

'Creative expectations and their resultant **Enlightened Responses** are based on awareness of all the available information. They are the culmination of a process that begins with self observation.'

Change your thoughts.
Change your life.
Change the world.

BODHI PALLANKA (THE PLACE OF ENLIGHTENMENT)
PRINCE SIDDHARTHA ATTAINED BUDDHAHOOD (FULL ENLIGHTEN-
MENT) IN THE YEAR 623 B C ON THE VAISAKHA FULL MOONDAY
SITTING UNDER THIS PEEPUL (BODHI) TREE.
THE VAJRASANA OR THE DIAMOND THRONE WHICH IS UNDER
THIS BUDHI TREE IS THE CENTRAL PLACE OF WORSHIP.

Ross hoping for instant enlightenment under Buddha's Bodhi Tree. India,1992.

CHAPTER FIFTEEN

AND FINALLY...

The preceding chapters have been filled with a collection of ideas, concepts, anecdotes and practical examples of how I have begun to make sense of my world. I believe self observation has taught me a great deal about the way I interact with my environment and those with whom I share it. It is my hope that you might experiment with the information and practical exercises provided and by so doing enhance your own experience of your own life.

I'd like to paraphrase a few lines from the opening paragraphs of this book, with an emphasis on how these thoughts can be applied to ALL the aspects of our lives, including our relationships with beings that have a different view of the world to ours. That should just about include everybody and every living and non-living thing!

'The Enlightened Response is about creating a peaceful, fulfilling and productive life, not only amidst or in spite of the daily turmoil, but because of it, accepting its inevitability, along with the inevitability of constant change.'

Self-observation – in various forms ranging from mundane chores to life-changing events – will lead to awareness. Awareness will give me resource material for building multi-creative expectations on which I can base my Enlightened Responses to any situation. Awareness will also open the windows of my perception and enhance my ability to objectively evaluate the events of my life.

And finally, I offer you a greeting that is common in India and Nepal. It is a word you will hear maybe a hundred times a day while travelling in the Himalaya and it has had special significance for me since my first trip to the region in 1992. It roughly translates to:

'I salute the divinity in you. I salute that special part of you which is not your behaviour or your beliefs. I salute that part of you which is of Light and Love, for when you are in that place in you, and I am in that place in me, we are one.'

And when I habitually react rather than choose to respond; when I meet someone who pushes my buttons; someone whose beliefs or behaviour I find difficult to accept; someone with whom I desire to create harmony; I silently recite this greeting while focussing in their direction. It helps me to see the side of them obscured by masks, behaviours, patterns and personalities – theirs and mine – and to see the heart of the child from whence they grew. It puts me in touch with my own purity, hidden somewhere beneath the collection of characteristics who others see as me.

Namaste

(Na-ma-stay)

THE ENLIGHTENED RESPONSE SUITE

Powerful Workshops
and Seminars written and facilitated by Ross Page

'It is always exciting when you come across someone or something that changes your view of life. To describe Ross and this book in such a way, is no exaggeration.'

LEATHAM GREEN,
HEAD OF ORGANISATIONAL DEVELOPMENT,
EAST SUSSEX COUNTY COUNCIL

What do other clients say?

"…unique style, personality and creative approach…" " …training methods that work." "…creates an ideal learning environment…" "…acclaimed by many as a major turning point in their lives…" "…quirky sense of humour. " "…outstanding course and a brilliant trainer." "445 out of 450 of our managers, reported that they would recommend the course."

**An ENLIGHTENED RESPONSE would be to call
and find out why people are saying these things
about Enlightened Response workshops.**

Enlightened Response workshops employ dynamic and interactive training techniques such as Experiential Learning, Accelerated Learning Techniques and Neuro Linguistic Programming.

Course titles include:

The Enlightened Response to: Getting what you want in life and business; Lifestyle Balance; Personal Excellence; Business Relationships; Triple 'A' Leadership; Tremendous Teams; The Stress/Success Balance; Powerful Presentations; Creative Thinking; Leading Change; Time Travel; Meeting Mastery; Caring for Customers; Transparent Training and Self-Centred Selling.

Open seminars also available on various topics focussing on Health and Happiness, Lifestyle Balance, and Creating the Life you Want – moment to moment, choice by choice.

For more information about
The Enlightened Response Suite of Workshops please contact us by:

Email : rosspage@enlightenedresponse.com

Telephone: +44 (0)7740 610199

Or visit our website: www.enlightenedresponse.com

ROSS PAGE
Life, learning and highlights

Since 1985 Ross has written and delivered training programmes for such diverse groups as senior corporate management, shop floor teams, the health resort industry, long term unemployed, ex-prisoners, foreign English students and parents of young children. Equally at home in the training room or on outdoor challenge activities, he has also led abseiling courses, hiking expeditions, team challenge camping trips, life-changing journeys of self observation and has trekked to an altitude of 19000 feet in the Nepal Himalaya.

Originally from Sydney, Australia, Ross now resides with his wife Diane in rural West Sussex, UK. He has two adult children; a daughter still residing in Australia and a son in Brighton, East Sussex. Like the song 'I'm a Citizen', one of 20 which he composed and recorded recently for the Human Values Foundation, Ross considers himself to be a 'citizen of planet earth'. He has a passion for assisting people to understand each other, which is reflected in his book, 'The Enlightened Response', and the similarly titled suite of personal development workshops.

Ross's wide assortment of businesses and salaried positions has provided a firm foundation for understanding and balancing the Wheel of Life, which combines well with his ability to teach these skills to others. His career path has included a restaurant, a tour coach company, freelance photographic business, marketing and promotions, resort management and many years performing as a solo singer and songwriter.

A qualified masseur, breath and body harmony therapist, Reiki practitioner, Enneagram facilitator and meditation instructor, Ross's workshops on Lifestyle Balance have been acclaimed as thought provoking and life changing.

He also has a passion for travel that has taken him to more than 30 countries. He cites his favourite trip as being his 10000mile, 5 month odyssey to the major holy cities of India, the snow-capped peaks of Nepal and to the teachings of the Dalai Lama at his home in exile in Himachal Pradesh in the foothills of the Himalaya.

And the journey continues…